Ivan Kiselev

Aspect-Oriented Programming with AspectJ

SAMS

201 West 103rd Street, Indianapolis, Indiana 46290

Aspect-Oriented Programming with AspectJ

International Standard Book Number: 0-672-32410-5

Library of Congress Catalog Card Number: 752063324103

Printed in the United States of America

First Printing: July 2002

05 04 03 02   4 3 2 1

Trademarks

Warning and Disclaimer

Executive Editor
Michael Stephens

Acquisitions Editor
Carol Ackerman

Development Editor
Tiffany Taylor

Managing Editor
Charlotte Clapp

Project Editor
George E. Nedeff

Copy Editor
Chip Gardner

Indexer
Sandra Henselmeier

Proofreader
Suzanne Thomas

Technical Editor
Ed Peters

Team Coordinator
Lynne Williams

Multimedia Developer
Dan Scherf

Interior Designer
Gary Adair

Cover Designer
Alan Clements

Contents at a Glance

Table of Contents

About the Author

Ivan Kiselev has over 20 years of software engineering and business experience. He is a chief technology officer at APP Design Group, Inc., a software company. Previously, Mr. Kiselev held technology leadership positions with a number of other software, financial, and telecommunication companies.

Mr. Kiselev is a senior-level architect and technologist with extensive experience in analysis, architecture, and development of large-scale, distributed information systems, as well as a recognized expert in object-oriented technology, the Internet, and EDI. Mr. Kiselev takes particular interest in applications of reusable frameworks and application servers to electronic commerce systems and development environments, as well as integrating scripting languages into all of these. Most of his efforts are devoted to architecture of distributed enterprise scale applications for the Web-based environment where he advocates a very pragmatic approach to system development.

Mr. Kiselev served on the ANSI C++ Standardization Committee from 1991–1993 and published over 20 articles and white papers in *Dr. Dobb's Journal*, *Java Developer's Journal*, *Software Development Magazine*, and other publications. Mr. Kiselev is a member of the Association for Computer Machinery and the Institute of Electrical and Electronics Engineers.

Dedication

To my wife and muse Lilia, and to my mom and dad without whom nothing would be possible.

Acknowledgments

Come on, nobody reads acknowledgements in technical books! However, if you insist, I am more than willing to go along—this is actually my only chance to demonstrate any literary eloquence, as the rest of the text is quite dry and geeky. There are so many people who directly or indirectly participated in this project that thanking them all would be impossible, but I will try anyway.

First of all, I do not thank the Academy of Motion Picture Arts and Sciences—I am reasonably sure that they had nothing to do with this particular book. Second, I would like to express real thanks to the members of AspectJ development team who created this wonderful tool: Ron Bodkin, Bill Griswold, Erik Hilsdale, Jim Hugunin, Wes Isberg, Mik Kersten, and Gregor Kiczales. I wish them the best of luck in marketing the tool and the concept—I am doing my part—and I believe that every programmer will be better off if they succeed.

People at Sams Publishing deserve much more than my thanks—I hope that this book will make them money, so, please, buy your own copy if this one is someone else's. As far as acknowledgements go, here is the story. This book happened largely because of the advanced thinking of Michael Stephens, who had the foresight to recognize the true value of the aspect-oriented concept and committed to publishing what I believe is the first book on the subject. The combined efforts of the Sams team converted my foreign-accented techno-speak into readable English—the passive voice alone could take a whole page of thanks! For this and many other things I extend my deepest gratitude to Tiffany Taylor, Chip Gardner, George Nedeff, Carol Ackerman, and all the people at Sams with whom I did not have an opportunity to work directly. Very special thanks goes to Ed Peters who has found more bugs in the examples than I would ever be prepared to admit without blushing.

I am grateful to Dr. F. F. Satdarova who, more than 20 years ago, showed me what computers can do—my life has changed forever. I am profoundly indebted to professors M. A. Stremel and Yu. A. Krupin, who had to read and edit all the write-ups I produced early in my career and took the responsibility to beat it into my then young and stupid head that writing is one of the most important skills that an engineer can posses. The lessons are still with me; thanks.

Finally, my family gave me the opportunity to write this book and tolerated my crazy schedule for so long. I will make up for it, I promise.

We Want to Hear from You!

As the reader of this book, *you* are our most important critic and commentator. We value your opinion and want to know what we're doing right, what we could do better, what areas you'd like to see us publish in, and any other words of wisdom you're willing to pass our way.

As an executive editor for Sams Publishing, I welcome your comments. You can email or write me directly to let me know what you did or didn't like about this book—as well as what we can do to make our books better.

Please note that I cannot help you with technical problems related to the *topic* of this book. We do have a User Services group, however, where I will forward specific technical questions related to the book.

When you write, please be sure to include this book's title and author as well as your name, email address, and phone number. I will carefully review your comments and share them with the author and editors who worked on the book.

Email: feedback@samspublishing.com

Mail: Michael Stephens
          Executive Editor
          Sams Publishing
          201 West 103rd Street
          Indianapolis, IN 46290 USA

For more information about this book or another Sams Publishing title, visit our Web site at www.samspublishing.com. Type the ISBN (excluding hyphens) or the title of a book in the Search field to find the page you're looking for.

Introduction

One gloomy Chicago evening I came across a collection of articles entitled "Aspect-Oriented Programming" in the *Communications of ACM* magazine.

Two things immediately struck me as odd: First, the concept was absolutely brilliant; second, I had never heard of it. I could deal with the second oddity: Although I'm an avid reader, it's impossible to keep on top of everything—if it escaped my attention, I just needed to catch up. But the brilliance was absolutely unexpected. The scale of it and its potential impact on everything I do professionally, as well as the entire software-engineering field, was so staggering that I would expect it to be included in every contemporary computer science course. Yet, nobody I asked had ever heard of it.

Then, I considered the weight of this discovery in historical perspective: What, in my memory, was the best idea in software since sliced bread? Object-oriented programming, which is as sliced as it gets as far as engineering disciplines are concerned. The first usable implementation of the object-oriented concept is traditionally attributed to the Simula-68 language, in the late 1960s. The first time we had a chance to use object-oriented concepts commercially on a real production project for which real people paid real money was in late 1980s, at the beginning of the telecom boom, when C++ was gaining ground on C and COBOL.

The bad news is that it took almost a quarter of a century for the last brilliant idea to enter the mainstream. The good news is that it all happened in the last century. This century will be different, and for that reason I wrote this book. I wrote it in a hope that by the time you read this, several other books will be available on the subject and the concept of aspect-oriented programming will be on its way to winning the support of millions of software developers around the world. I hope that we won't have to wait another quarter century for the next great concept, hopefully it will appear sooner, be better, and move us further.

Of course, there are more prosaic reasons for the relative obscurity of aspect-oriented programming. One of them is that like most new ideas, it was confined to academic circles for a while. This book is an attempt to present a showcase of aspects for practicing software engineers such as myself, so you will not find a complete syntax analysis, a 400-plus citations reference section, or any other attributes of a classic treatise in this book. In this book, expect to find examples. Lots of them. Simple and complex, short and long, meticulously explained, and mentioned in passing. So you can cut and paste, see and do, notice and remember.

My sincere hope is that after reading this book your programming will never be the same, and you will find thousands more uses for the concepts illustrated here. You will create an infinite kaleidoscope of patterns that will make your next project smaller, cheaper, and more reliable. And, hopefully, you will sell a lot of whatever you are programming—ultimately, it is all about money and you will make more of it. Let the journey begin.

The Intended Audience

The purpose of this book is to introduce the concept of aspect-oriented programming and the AspectJ tool and show their benefits in designing Java-based, large-scale information systems with crosscutting concerns. I present a new concept and a new tool that works with it. Neither part of this duo is emphasized enough to make this book a definitive reference for either one. This book deploys a geeky concept of playing with toys that can roughly be described as the following:

1. Here is an idea—aspect-oriented programming.

2. This is the tool—AspectJ.

3. Let's see what can be done with these two.

In other words, the intent is to tease professional programmers with possibilities that aspects afford them.

I expect the reader to be proficient with Java and its popular APIs, especially Java Database Connectivity (JDBC) and servlets. Some familiarity with principles of Web development and multithreaded programming will also be very helpful. The book will most benefit engineers who have been through large-scale development projects or intend to embark on one. The majority of the book is devoted to a Web-based example application, so if you are in Web development, you can find some benefits for it, too.

Organization

Part I, "Introduction to Programming with AspectJ," introduces the idea of aspect-oriented programming (AOP): how it came to be, what problems it solves, and how these problems were solved (or unsolved) by pre-AOP methods. The text explains basic techniques of AOP, why they are useful on a purely intuitive level, and what their relationships with object-oriented programming are. It also introduces the AspectJ language and compiler; one simple example is considered in detail.

Part II, "Strategies for a Real Application," is the main section of the book. A small, but realistic Web application that uses popular Java APIs is developed for illustration. The application's crosscutting concerns are used as showcases for AspectJ at work.

Part III, "Language Details," contains more information about the AspectJ language with the emphasis on features not used in the previous parts.

Part IV, "Conclusion," discusses emerging use patterns and provides some additional information about tools used in this book: Ant, Tomcat, and MySQL. The information about AspectJ command-line tools and API is also provided here.

What Is Not Here

I deliberately omitted two important pieces of the AspectJ tool chest: AspectJ debugger and AspectJ support for various development environments. The reasons are as follows. First, the debugger is still being actively developed at the time of this writing and the up-to-date information available online will be more accurate. Second, various add-ons are not essential to the concepts presented here, although, they do make life a little easier. Currently, there is support for Borland's JBuilder, Sun's Forte, and Emacs. There are also some rumors about possible Eclipse integration. The IDE tool selection is a personal choice anyway, so, for the purposes of this book any text editor would do just fine.

I also did not describe in detail privileged aspects—a feature that I consider quite dangerous.

Conventions

Several typefaces are utilized throughout this book. Monotype constant-width font is used for

- Directory paths and filenames

- URLs and host names

- Entities related to code (class names, variables, and so on) used within the text

- Code examples

- XML fragments, elements, and tags

- Operating system (shell) level commands

Examples

All examples in this book are available online at the Sams Publishing Web site `http://www.samspublishing.com`.

In the examples listed in the text, the code was slightly formatted to fit the printed page. Source code control tags were also deleted to save space. Other than that, the examples in the book should be exactly as the code available online.

Although I'm perfectly willing to blame anyone else for bugs in the examples, I nevertheless accept the full responsibility for them and will be thankful if they are reported to `feedback@samspublishing.com`. It is also worth reminding you that the examples are provided as is without any warranties whatsoever, expressed or implied.

All examples were compiled and tested with version 1.0 of the AspectJ tool. The version information for the rest of the tools used to run the examples is contained in the appendixes.

PART I

Introduction to Programming with AspectJ

IN THIS PART

And the eternally tragic aspect of the drama lies in this: that the problem set before us is one the elements of which can be but imperfectly known, and of which even an approximately right solution rarely presents itself, until that stern critic, aged experience, has been furnished with ample justification for venting his sarcastic humor upon the irreparable blunders we have already made.

—Thomas Henry Huxley, *Aphorisms and Reflections*, selected by Henrietta A. Huxley. Reflection #227.

1

Why Aspect-Oriented Programming?

In this chapter, we will discuss how aspect-oriented programming is connected to the previously existing methods and what kind of problems it is designed to solve. The goal here is to provide an intuitive understanding of the concept without diving into technical details.

Complexity Management

Humans are industrious creatures. If the load on our back gets too heavy we invent the wheel. As soon as a pair of wheels is not sufficient anymore, we put another pair in front and call it a wagon. If the wagon cannot keep up in the fast-paced Stone Age, we enlist a horse to help (granted, a horse has never volunteered). I do not claim to have witnessed the progress of a simple cart or that it happened exactly as described, but we certainly made some progress in constructing mechanical devices to move a load.

I did witness the development of modern programming techniques—including computers, languages, compilers, methodologies, CAD and RAD tools, and so on. The early computers could do very, very simple arithmetic operations and branching on conditions.

The invention of the auto-code and assembly languages was a big breakthrough—you could actually read the program and have a reasonable idea what it was supposed to do. Forcing it to do that was another problem, but it became feasible to code rather complex algorithms and still maintain comprehension of what was happening.

The real economic impact came with the appearance of so-called business languages (COBOL, Algol, and so on) and computers that could support them. These languages bridged the gap between engineers and business folks: A person without special training in engineering could solve a business problem using a computer! The achievement was so great that, in my humble opinion, it stalled the development of the whole field for at least 20 years.

Minicomputers were born next, with PCs following shortly after. Tools such as SQL, xBase, and other fourth-generation languages allowed coding business problems for smaller machines by individual programmers or small teams thereof.

And then it hit us: Everything we did up to that point was about quantity—faster computers, more memory, quicker turnaround, more data in the database—until we produced a huge load of legacy applications. It got us thinking: If we kept expressing our business problems linearly, the way computers understood them at the time, increasing the computer's speed would not do us any good. Humans were the limiting factor; we had to translate our domain knowledge into linear sets of instructions. If we could make a computer understand how the world looks, the computer could do most of the translations. The world looks like data that's closely associated with actions, and we now call these things *objects*.

That simple-and-easy-to-implement idea was one of the most powerful inventions ever. Modern programmers became pretty good at decomposing our surroundings into objects. There are numerous methodologies available to guide you, tools to translate your thoughts into executable code, business processes to achieve unbelievable efficiencies in turning problems into opportunities. Yet we are hitting the wall again.

Our object-oriented systems model problem domains beautifully, as long as you manage to stay within the domain. Our object-oriented systems can grow quite large, as long as you do not cross an invisible size boundary when they become as fragile as glass castles. Our object-oriented systems can be made open and extendable, as long as you guard its interfaces from ever changing. Our object-oriented systems do support collaborative development efforts, as long as your company can keep the turnover low. Our knowledge of the world gets captured into elegantly constructed "standard" libraries—from STL to EJB—as long you are willing to keep up with the proliferation of the alphabet soup.

In other words, the degree of complexity of business problems that can be solved efficiently using object-oriented techniques is about to achieve its maximum. We have to keep thinking.

From OO to Aspects

In several situations, object-oriented programming becomes particularly painful. First, there is a fundamental confinement of object-oriented models to a particular problem domain. For instance, what you have done for an insurance company is useless for a combat modeling because your insurance policy object does not behave like a tank no matter how hard you are trying to militarize—I mean to generalize—it. In addition, some problems are not attached to any particular problem domain—they spread across them, affect everybody, and we just keep writing code to address them over and over again. And this code creeps all over our nicely constructed object models.

Second, objects have notoriously fragile outer shells (the interfaces), and designers are forced to make interface decisions early or face the consequences. As long as interfaces remain intact, everybody is happy—but business moves, problems change, and new issues arise. Pity the guy who changes the interface—everybody has to know about it, and a lot of code has to be touched. And yet object-oriented development methods assume the knowledge of all needed interfaces for the developer.

Consider the following artificial example. One company is involved in dealing with apples, grapes, oranges, DVD players, loud speakers, and TV sets. It naturally leads to two object hierarchies: one for fruits and another for gadgets (see Figure 1.1).

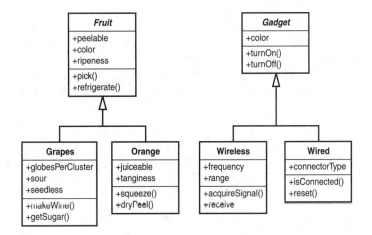

FIGURE 1.1   Disparate object hierarchies.

Besides being things, fruits and gadgets also interact with the rest of the world—they can act (or can be acted upon) as commodities or be packaged and stored. This requires an extension of the model to include properties and behavior characteristics of the respective new objects. Thus, making fruits and gadgets inherit these properties or behaviors or, in case of single inheritance environment, implement required interfaces (see Figure 1.2).

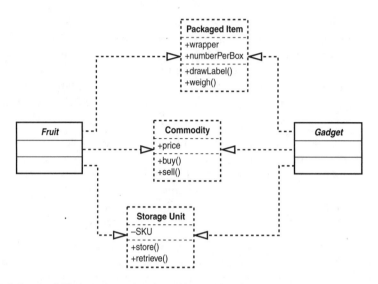

FIGURE 1.2   Real-life interfaces for domain-specific objects.

It is very important to notice that newly introduced interfaces have nothing to do with the original object's problem domain. A gadget's operation does not relate in any meaningful way to our desire to trade it, store it, or shrink-wrap it. A second important consideration is that to implement these desired traits, the designer of the fruit and gadget objects must be concerned with their commodity's features from day one if not earlier.

From a businessperson's point of view, a storage or packaging feature of a commodity does not really relate to any particular commodity: from fruits to gadgets, it's all the same set of concerns. The concerns' independence of a problem domain makes them crosscutting (see Figure 1.3).

Grapes	Orange	Wireless	Wired	
+makeWine()	+squeeze()	+acquireSignal()	+isConnected()	
+getSugar()	+dryPeel()	+receive()	+reset()	
+drawLabel()	+drawLabel()	+drawLabel()	+drawLabel()	*Packaged Item*
+weigh()	+weigh()	+weigh()	+weigh()	
+buy()	+buy()	+buy()	+buy()	*Commodity*
+sell()	+sell()	+sell()	+sell()	
+store()	+store()	+store()	+store()	*Storage Unit*
+retrieve()	+retrieve()	+retrieve()	+retrieve()	

FIGURE 1.3   Crosscutting concerns.

Of course, these concerns can be addressed with existing object-oriented tools, for example, by implementing or inheriting all relevant features. The big problem with this approach is a necessity to do all the implementation work up front, whereas in real life many concerns might not even be known until much later.

In a simplistic view of object-oriented programming, we tell the computer to bundle chunks of data with pointers to functions and keep it along with all inherited objects from this point backward. Theoretically, the computer does not care how we bundle—in object-oriented programming we do it vertically, that is, common attributes and behavior are encapsulated in the root object (objects `Fruit` and `Gadget` in Figure 1.1). In object-oriented languages we are explicitly indicating what should be bundled by means of inheritance and, again, we have to do it from the beginning. And computers dutifully generate all needed code to keep these bundles tied.

If our computers can do this, they should also be able to bundle things horizontally. For example, if we specify that fruits and gadgets are also packaged items that can be traded as commodities, and can be stored, there are no principal difficulties for a computer to examine all fruits and gadgets and add horizontal bundles to the existing vertical ones. The critical advantage horizontal bundling is that fruits, gadgets, or any other commodity our imaginary company will ever deal with, do not have to be aware of the bundling. From another point of view, if a packaging functionality will ever be coded, than it can be bundled to any object ever made without the object ever suspecting it. This will allow separation of domain-specific models, captured in traditional object hierarchies, from general concerns that span across them horizontally.

The previous example shows an application of a so-called static crosscutting technique where a computer is asked to find and modify existing object hierarchies. The whole concept of bundling can be taken a little further as long as a tool that finds existing code is available. For example, let's say there is a service that provides information delivery for its clients: pay-per-view TV, magazines, reprints, music on demand, and so on. Traditional implementation leads to classes shown in Figure 1.4.

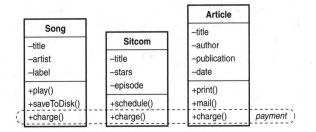

FIGURE 1.4   Content classes.

The provider of the service is naturally expecting to get paid for the content. This is why each class contains the charge method that deals with financial details peculiar to each piece of information sold. These charge methods are parts of the crosscutting payment concern, and implementing it as such will provide some undeniable benefits:

- Each charge method has to know whom to charge, and what payment method should be used in each particular case including, possibly, some credit arrangements.

- An implementer of a song class has to be concerned with money, which is distractive and disenchanting. It's better to ask the computer to find all the appropriate places in the methods that provide the content. Then charge the customer from one central financial "module" that will be fully aware of all monetary arrangements between the company and its customers. (Identifying the correct places is not trivial: For a song it would be after 51% of it was played or after 100% of it was saved to disk; for a sitcom it would be after it was scheduled and first episode delivered; for an article it would be after it was printed and mailed.)

In addition to a content delivery, the payment concern can extend to conditions or events. For example, a customer can be charged a subscription fee every month or given a referral credit for recommending the service to friends. So, the computer will need special markers to be found in the code for the whole approach to work. In the lingo of the tool described in this book—AspectJ—this technique of addressing concerns is called *dynamic crosscutting*, these markers are called *join points*, and the language construct that implements the concern is called an *aspect*.

Aspect-Oriented Programming

In brief, aspect-oriented programming is a technique to design and code (in other words, to address) crosscutting business concerns. Note the difference: Object-oriented programming addresses common concerns; that is, attributes and behaviors common among related entities are captured on top of a class hierarchy. In contrast, aspect-oriented programming deals with unrelated items, trying to modularize their common attributes and behaviors in a software layer that spreads across classes regardless of domain, thus increasing modularity of the software.

Aspect-oriented programming promises to help us modularize some of the least exciting technical problems. Its idea is to separate concerns. The expressed (implemented) concern remains intact no matter how evolved the system gets; that is, the concern is separated from the main system. From another angle, the addressing of concerns (that is, the implementation of concern's logic in an aspect) can change dramatically without affecting the rest of the software. (At least, this is the theoretical promise.)

Aspect-oriented programming is an additional technique, not a replacement for object-oriented programming. As improvements in programming paradigms enabled the solution of more complex problems more effectively, the aspect-oriented method is just the next step in the same direction—another addition to the programmer's toolbox that will increase productivity. It gives us one more dimension to slice and dice (or, to use a proper term, modularize) our problems. But how do we know what is object and what is aspect? The object-oriented programming discipline worked out very strong links to the human cognitive process. Remember, inheritance is a reflection of "is" relationships, and association models of "has" relationships. Aspect-oriented programming is too young to have such solid recipes; designers must rely on their discretion to decompose the problem effectively. The simplified rule of thumb was expressed in an early paper on aspect-oriented programming (by Kiczales et al; see Appendix F, "References," for more information):

> "...a property that must be implemented is
>
> - A component, if it can be cleanly encapsulated in a generalized procedure (that is object, method, procedure, API). By cleanly, we mean well localized, and easily accessed and composed as necessary. Components tend to be units of the system's functional decomposition, such as image filters, bank accounts, and GUI widgets.
>
> - An aspect, if it can not be cleanly encapsulated in a generalized procedure. Aspects tend not to be units of the system's functional decomposition, but rather to be properties that affect the performance or semantics of the components in systemic ways. Examples of aspects include memory access patterns and synchronization of concurrent objects."

As in the case with object hierarchy or, more generally, with overall system architecture, the proper modularization is, in many respects, a matter of a design skill rather than a formal methodology. The same is true with aspects and, more generally, with crosscutting concerns. Ultimately, it becomes a decision based on a combination of usage patterns and the designer's experience.

Meet AspectJ

Why Java? Well, there are benefits to an elegant, pure object-oriented, portable, runtime language that gains popularity fast. The discussion of Java's merits deserves a separate book, but for the purposes of aspect-oriented programming Java has two distinct advantages: popularity and introspection API.

AspectJ is an open-source tool developed at Xerox PARC (see Appendix E for project details). It finds special markers (also known as *join points*) in the Java source code and bundles the source with the separately developed modules called *aspects*—hence the name. To do its job AspectJ uses a special extension to the Java language that enables the development of these special aspect modules.

AspectJ is the easiest way to get aquatinted with aspect-oriented programming. Its biggest practical advantage is the support for evolutionary development: dive in or get wet slowly depending on your requirements. It has politically motivated development options: compiling aspects in or out with your existing code base—as described earlier, it finds special places in the source code, and new code inserted at these places can be removed if required by the existing organizational procedures. Several development alternatives are available including aspects as development aids, ancillary add-ons, or part of a core design. Developers can choose adoption strategies most suited for their development organizations—from grass roots to the corner office—benefits of properly addressed concerns can be demonstrated on any size project.

Briefly, aspect-oriented programming with AspectJ works like this: You develop Java classes that reflect your business logic, and then you develop aspects that address your crosscutting concerns. Whether you develop objects and aspects together or separately, sequentially, or in parallel is a matter of your development strategy that will be discussed in Part II of the book. The important thing is that after you are done, you compile the whole application with the AspectJ compiler; it does all the horizontal bundling in pure Java, and then produces executable byte codes. Of course, there is more to it than described in this paragraph, but we have the whole book ahead to explain the gory details.

Summary

Aspect-oriented ideas were developed in response to ever increasing complexities of business problems that programmers are called to solve. It represents a natural evolution of programming paradigms that allow modularizing units of work in order to keep up with the workload. Aspect-oriented programming is designed to help solve a specific class of problems that exhibit crosscutting properties, those that cannot be elegantly solved within a particular domain and/or object structure.

Next, we will look at what it all means in practice: How the AspectJ tool helps to implement the aspect-oriented ideas in the context of a real program.

2

A First Look at AspectJ

In this chapter, we will take our first look at the AspectJ language and compiler and will see how the concept works. We will consider a very simple example, but its simplicity will allow us to take a backstage tour of the inner working of the tool.

Quick Setup Guide

- To get started, you need the Java software development kit (which I assume you've already installed) and the AspectJ binary distribution. The former is available from Sun at `http://java.sun.com`, the latter from the AspectJ home site at `http://www.aspectj.org`. The AspectJ distribution contains several tools, but for this chapter only the AspectJ compiler (ajc) is needed. Installation and set up does not present any particular challenge, but two things have to be taken care of after installation is complete:

- The AspectJ runtime library `<aspectj_dir>/lib/aspectjrt.jar` should be added to the class path.

- The AspectJ `<aspectj_dir>/bin` directory should be added to the path.

The `README-TOOLS.htm` file contains platform-specific instructions. Generally, AspectJ should be able to run anywhere Java 2 is supported.

AspectJ documentation recommends placing aspect-specific source code into files with the suffix `.java`. This convention will be followed for the examples presented in the book. Finally, all source files needed for compilation must be specified in the ajc command line; unlike javac it does not search for classes automatically.

Introduction to the Language

AspectJ extends Java with several new concepts. The core is the *aspect*—the basic unit of modularity, the embodiment of the application's concerns. For the purposes of this chapter, it is easier to consider an aspect to be an aspect-oriented equivalent of a class; the differences will be emphasized later. The aspect is defined by the keyword aspect and this is all you need to know to produce a "Hello, world!" program.

```java
package intro;
import java.io.*;

public aspect HelloWorldA
{
    public static void main(String args[])
    {
        System.out.println("Hello, world!");
    }
}
```

To compile and execute the program, run the following commands:

```
>ajc intro/HelloWorldA.java
>java intro.HelloWordlA
```

The program should print "Hello, world!" text to the standard output. It is not that exciting yet, but, on a positive side, it indicates that the AspectJ environment is installed and working correctly. I also assume that a Java executable is in the path.

Aspects might have methods, fields, and some other attributes of a class, but their main purpose is to hold *pointcuts*, *advices*, and *introductions*. These are all new concepts that do not have logical equivalents in standard Java.

Join Points

Special well-defined points in the program flow (previously described as *markers* or *join points*) are needed where horizontal bundling occurs in the code. AspectJ defines 11 types of such join points that can be recognized by the compiler. They include method calls, exception execution, field assignment, and so on; there is a special syntax for each.

Pointcuts

To specify which join points are interesting in a particular situation, you define a pointcut, which selects certain join points along with some context values specific to these points.

Advices

When all interesting join points are described in pointcuts, it's time to add some executable code, which will be an actual implementation of a concern. It is called an *advice* and it gets executed when a given pointcut is reached. Of course, there are twists to that, too. The advice's code can be told to run before join points are reached, after, or instead of them if so desired.

Consider the following examples. In Listings 2.1 and 2.2, two classes of unrelated object hierarchies are presented.

LISTING 2.1   Class A

```java
package intro;

public class A
{
    int a(int x)
    {
        System.out.println("method 'A.a'");
        return b(x);
    }

    int b(int x)
    {
        System.out.println("method 'A.b'");
        c("x");
        return x;
    }

    String c(String x)
    {
        System.out.println("method 'A.c'");
        (new B()).c(3.14);
        return x;
    }

    public static void main(String args[])
    {
```

LISTING 2.1   Continued

```
    try
    {
        A t = new A();

        System.out.println("Start of "+t.getClass().getName());

        t.a(5);

        System.out.println("End of "+t.getClass().getName());
    }
    catch(Throwable t)
    {
        System.out.println("Exception in main:"+t);
        t.printStackTrace(System.out);
    }
  }
}
```

LISTING 2.2   Class B

```
package intro;

public class B
{
    void c(double x)
    {
        System.out.println("method 'B.c'");
    }
}
```

Class A has the main() and three other methods with different signatures; class B has only one method. All methods of both classes do nothing useful, but print out their respective names. An aspect Showcase presented in Listing 2.3 contains three point-cuts and three advices.

LISTING 2.3   Aspect Showcase.java

```
package intro;

public aspect Showcase
{
```

LISTING 2.3   Continued

```
pointcut int_A_a_int():   call(int A.a(int));
pointcut int_A_all_int(): call(int A.*(int));
pointcut all_all_c_all(): call(* *.c(*));

before(): int_A_a_int()
{
    System.out.println("Before: " + thisJoinPoint);
}

after(): int_A_all_int() || all_all_c_all()
{
    System.out.println("After: " + thisJoinPoint);
}

Object around(): all_all_c_all()
{
    System.out.println("Start around: " + thisJoinPoint);
    Object o = proceed();
    System.out.println("End around: " + thisJoinPoint);
    return o;
}
}
```

All its pointcuts are method call pointcuts defined for various method signatures:

- `int_A_a_int()` picks a join point when a method call to a method `int a(int)` of class `A` is made.

- `int_A_all_int()` picks join points of method calls for all methods of class `A` having the same signature `int *(int)`, where `*` denotes "anything" as the method name. There are two such methods, both are in class `A`: `int A.a(int)` and `int A.b(int)`.

- `all_all_c_all()` picks all methods named `c` of all classes with any signature. There are two such methods: `String A.c(String)` and `void B.c(double)`.

The aspect `Showcase` also contains all three possible kinds of advice (it is possible to have more advices, but there are still three basic kinds):

- The `before` advice of the `Showcase` aspect will run before the `int_A_a_int()` pointcut's join points, in this particular case, before all calls to `int A.a(int)` method.

- The `after` advice will run after one of the join points of either
`int_A_all_int()` or `all_all_c_all()` pointcuts, in this example, after methods
`void intro.B.c(double)`, `String intro.A.c(String)`, `int intro.A.b(int)`, or
`int intro.A.a(int)` will finish.

- The around advice will run instead of all join points picked by the
`all_all_c_all()` pointcut. It means that when such a join point is reached,
the control will be passed to the advice, and then it can decide what to do. In
the example on Listing 2.4 the advice just executes whatever was originally
intended by a special `proceed()` keyword. In the example this happens for
methods `String intro.A.c(String)` and `void intro.B.c(double)`—that is, for
all methods named c affected by this aspect regardless of signature.

The code of the advices uses a special variable `thisJointPoint`. It is bound to an
object that contains the context for the advice's current join point. In this example it
is used just to print the join point name. This and other special variables are part of
the AspectJ reflection API (see Appendix A, "AspectJ API," for details).

The sources can be compiled with or without the `Showcase` aspect. Nothing in classes
A and B suggests that the aspect event exists. So, if the classes are compiled with the
following command

```
>ajc intro/A.java intro/B.java
```

the program can be run as

```
>java intro.A
```

and produces the following output:

```
Start of intro.A
method 'A.a'
method 'A.b'
method 'A.c'
method 'B.c'
End of intro.A
```

It shows the call stack trace as intended: from `main()` to `B.c()`. When classes A, B,
and the aspect `Showcase` are compiled together with this command

```
>ajc intro/A.java intro/B.java intro/Showcase.java
```

and the class A is run, the output should resemble the following:

```
Start of intro.A
Before: call(int intro.A.a(int))
method 'A.a'
method 'A.b'
Start around: call(String intro.A.c(String))
method 'A.c'
Start around: call(void intro.B.c(double))
method 'B.c'
After: call(void intro.B.c(double))
End around: call(void intro.B.c(double))
After: call(String intro.A.c(String))
End around: call(String intro.A.c(String))
After: call(int intro.A.b(int))
After: call(int intro.A.a(int))
End of intro.A
```

In addition to the method's output, the output from the aspect's advices can also be seen. Table 2.1 helps to analyze the chain of events.

TABLE 2.1   Output Breakdown

	Call Sequence	Pointcut	Advise	Output
1	main(String[])			Start of intro.A
2	int intro.A.a(int)	int_A_a_int()	before	Before: call(int intro.A.a(int)) method 'A.a'
3	int intro.A.b(int)	int_A_all_int()		method 'A.b'
4	String intro.A.c(String)	all_all_c_all()	around	Start around: call(String intro.A.c(String)) method 'A.c'
5	Void intro.B.c(double)	all_all_c_all()	around after	Start around: call(void intro.B.c(double)) method 'B.c' After: call(void intro.B.c(double))

TABLE 2.1   Continued

	Call Sequence	Pointcut	Advise	Output
				End around:
				call(void
				intro.B.c(double))
6	String intro.A.c(String)	all_all_c_all()	around	After: call(String
			after	intro.A.c(String))
				End around:
				call(String
				intro.A.c(String))
7	int intro.A.b(int)	int_A_all_int()	after	After: call(int
				intro.A.b(int))
8	int intro.A.a(int)	int_A_all_int()	after	After: call(int
				intro.A.a(int))
9	main(String[])			End of intro.A

The rows in the table are as follows:

- The output begins with main's message (row 1).

- As soon as a call to A.a() is placed in main() the before advise gets executed (row 2) because int_A_a_int() pointcut picks the call to A.a(). The A.a() method's trace output follows it (also row 2).

- The pointcut int_A_all_int() picks a call from A.a() to A.b(), but no advice's output happens because this pointcut is bound to the after advice; its output is present when both methods picked out by it (A.a() and A.b()) are complete (rows 7 and 8).

- On row 4 is the output from the around advice that gets triggered on calls to A.c(). The matching output—the end of the same around advice—is on row 6.

- Row 5 shows the lifecycle of the method B.c(): Starting with the around advice it proceeds to trace output, then to the end of the same around advice, and finishes with the after advice—all picked by the same pointcut all_all_c_all(). The same analysis applies to row 6; two advices are triggered by the same pointcut.

How It All Works

It is now time to reveal the magic behind AspectJ or, more precisely, that there is no magic. In saying so, I'm not undermining the sheer ingenuity of the AspectJ authors—it is a brilliant implementation of a truly innovative concept—the goal here is to demonstrate the mechanics of it to gain fuller understanding of how the tool works.

To ask ajc to spill its guts, issue the following command:

```
>ajc -preprocess intro/A.java intro/B.java intro/Showcase.java
```

In response, ajc will produce a set of greatly expanded Java files and stop without compiling them into byte codes. These files can be found in the ./ajworkingdir subdirectory. This subdirectory, in our case, will contain the same three files: A.java, B.java, and Showcase.java. Closer examination shows that this is pretty much the limit of the resemblance. Listing 2.4 shows what the Showcase aspect has turned into.

LISTING 2.4   Compiled Aspect Showcase

```
package intro;
public class Showcase
{
    public final void
      before0$ajc(org.aspectj.lang.JoinPoint.StaticPart
      thisJoinPointStaticPart)
    {
        System.out.println("Before: " + thisJoinPointStaticPart);
    }

    public final void
      after0$ajc(org.aspectj.lang.JoinPoint.StaticPart
      thisJoinPointStaticPart)
    {
        System.out.println("After: " + thisJoinPointStaticPart);
    }

    public Showcase()
    {
        super();
    }
    public static Showcase aspect$;
    public static Showcase aspectOf()
    {
```

LISTING 2.4 Continued

```
        return Showcase.aspect$;
    }

    public static boolean hasAspect()
    {
        return Showcase.aspect$ != null;
    }

    static
    {
        Showcase.aspect$ = new Showcase();
    }
}
```

First of all, it is now a normal Java class. Second, the body of the before and after advices are now normal instance methods called before0$ajc and after0$ajc, respectively, and each of them receive a join point context variable thisJoinPointStaticPart. The rest of it is ancillary code to support the AspectJ runtime system; it does not have anything to do with the original Showcase aspect per se. Notably absent are any mentions of pointcuts and the around advice.

After examining Listings 2.3 and 2.4 it becomes clear that pointcuts do not have to be within the Showcase class—ajc resolves them explicitly and places all necessary code directly at the join point, in the case of the B class—instead of the body of the method B.c().

As you can see in Figure 2.1, now method B.c() is an exact copy of Showcase's original around advice with the proceed() keyword replaced by the c$ajcPostAround6$ajcVoidWrapper() method call. The latter calls c$ajcPostAround6() and it, in turn, does two things: executes the original B.c() method wrapped in c$ajcPostCall and calls Showcase's after advice via newly generated Showcase.after0$ajc() method (see Listing 2.4 for the source). The static variable c$ajcjp1 provides the join point context—a call to a method with a signature void intro.B.c(double), in this particular case. The A class is essentially similar; the compilation result is just much longer because the class has more methods.

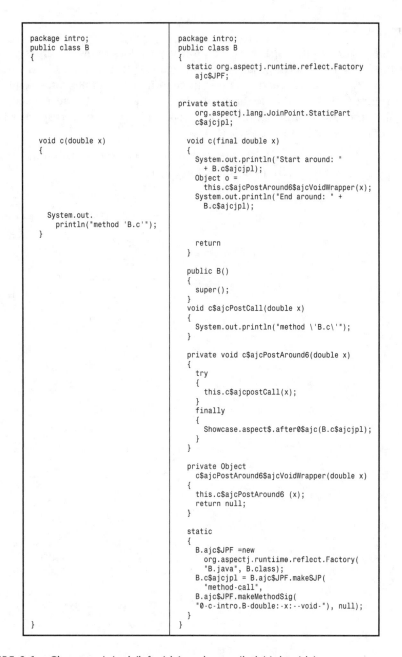

```
package intro;                    package intro;
public class B                    public class B
{                                 {
                                    static org.aspectj.runtime.reflect.Factory
                                      ajc$JPF;

                                    private static
                                      org.aspectj.lang.JoinPoint.StaticPart
                                      c$ajcjpl;

  void c(double x)                  void c(final double x)
  {                                 {
                                      System.out.println("Start around: "
                                        + B.c$ajcjpl);
                                      Object o =
                                        this.c$ajcPostAround6$ajcVoidWrapper(x);
                                      System.out.println("End around: " +
                                        B.c$ajcjpl);


    System.out.                       return
      println("method 'B.c'");     }
  }
                                    public B()
                                    {
                                      super();
                                    }
                                    void c$ajcPostCall(double x)
                                    {
                                      System.out.println("method \'B.c\'");
                                    }

                                    private void c$ajcPostAround6(double x)
                                    {
                                      try
                                      {
                                        this.c$ajcpostCall(x);
                                      }
                                      finally
                                      {
                                        Showcase.aspect$.after0$ajc(B.c$ajcjpl);
                                      }
                                    }

                                    private Object
                                      c$ajcPostAround6$ajcVoidWrapper(double x)
                                    {
                                      this.c$ajcPostAround6 (x);
                                      return null;
                                    }

                                    static
                                    {
                                      B.ajc$JPF =new
                                        org.aspectj.runtiime.reflect.Factory(
                                        "B.java", B.class);
                                      B.c$ajcjpl = B.ajc$JPF.makeSJP(
                                        "method-call",
                                        B.ajc$JPF.makeMethodSig(
                                        "0-c-intro.B-double:-x:--void-"), null);
                                    }
}                                 }
```

FIGURE 2.1   Class B: original (left side) and compiled (right side).

Summary

Compiling sources with AspectJ lets you introduce a lot of new and interesting functionality to the unsuspecting classes. In our example, a small class B was enhanced with two advices, which, theoretically, can be infinitely complex and useful. You can also see that there is indeed no magic involved—just a cleverly constructed set of compilation rules that instruct the AspectJ tool on how to process aspects with regard to the Java source code.

Now, after seeing the AspectJ tool at work and gaining some initial understanding of its internals, it is time to try to do something useful with it.

PART II

Strategies for a Real Application

IN THIS PART

Let us then suppose the mind to be, as we say, white paper, void of all characters, without any ideas; how comes it to be furnished...? To this I answer, in one word, from experience: in that, all our knowledge is founded; and from that it ultimately derives itself.

—John Locke, *An Essay Concerning Human Understanding*, bk. II, ch. 1

3

Application Description

In the following several chapters you will design and build a general-purpose e-zine called *AspectNews* that allows registered users to access published content via the Web and submit new stories. This chapter describes the application's architecture, tools, and development environment.

Business Requirements and Usage

The example application has the following business requirements:

- Customization—the system's functionality depends on users' identity. Users will subscribe for certain categories of stories and will be able to view them on demand.

- Security—the content will be available only to registered users.

- Robustness—the system will try to mimic the behavior of real production software with regard to reliability.

The typical usage scenario runs as follows:

1. A user hits the AspectNews Web site.

2. The application prompts the user with login information with an option to register unless the user is an existing customer.

3. The user either logs in or registers and is redirected to the start-up page.

4. From the start-up page the user can do one of the following: select news categories of interest, read news stories, or submit new news stories.

Although the application is somewhat simplistic from the functionality standpoint (this is on purpose—this book is not about Web application development), the intent is to make it literally production ready, with all major concerns addressed. And concerns are plentiful: uniform exception handling and reporting strategies, general improvement of modularity using aspect-specific design patterns, synchronization policies, pooling of limited resources (such as, database connections), global performance optimizations using automatic buffering, security, and so on. Despite its simplicity, the application will have three distinctive subsystems to demonstrate the crosscutting nature of our concerns: presentation logic, persistence layer, and security system, which itself, in turn, will be implemented as a crosscutting concern (don't you love recursion?).

Architecture

The general architecture is a classic three tier (see Figure 3.1): The client's layer is pure HTML; presentation and business logic are in Java Servlet Pages (JSPs), servlets, and server side class libraries; and data is in relational database.

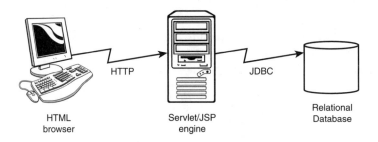

FIGURE 3.1   Here is the application's classic three-tier architecture.

The middle tier, business logic, breaks down into three subsystems of its own: output formatting, security, and persistence. Output formatting will be implemented using JSPs with custom tags. The persistence subsystem is represented by a layer of code that makes JDBC calls to the relational database. The security will be form-based with a database-based repository.

Tools

To implement the application you obviously need Java and AspectJ. In addition, I chose to use the following open source software:

- Tomcat JSP/Servlet engine
- MySQL relational database
- Ant build utility

There is no particular reason for any of the selections beside easy availability; anyone with enough patience can obtain, install, and configure them. Furthermore, any other servlet engine combined with a relational database that has a JDBC driver will do just fine, and a build tool is a matter of personal or organizational preference, anyway. Appendix C, "Auxiliary Tools," contains more details about these tools including version numbers, licensing, and configuration information.

File Layout

I don't expect you to type along, but playing with the examples can be an interesting part of the experience. In addition to building the example application, I've provided plenty of usage details regarding development and production builds with AspectJ and how to organize the structure of a project with aspects. So, let's begin with the source organization (see Figure 3.2).

The source tree contains several branches:

- src/—Java source files for all the business logic, security, persistence, and aspects. All Java source code is organized in packages; the directory structure down from this level corresponds to the package hierarchy as described here.

- web/—JSP pages for the AspectNews Web site. This is the document root of the AspectNews application.

- web/WEB-INF/—Configuration files for the application, including the Web application deployment descriptor and the tag library descriptor.

- build/—Temporary directory where the results of the build process are stored. This directory will be used to create a deployable copy of the AspectNews Web application.

- sql/—The directory for SQL scripts used to create and populate the database.

Java sources are divided into several packages:

- intro—for the examples shown in Part I of the book, "Introduction to Programming with AspectJ"

- db—for the database related classes

- security—for all security code

- tags—for all presentation JSP tags

- language—for the examples in Part III, "Language Details"

- wrong—for the examples that should not work

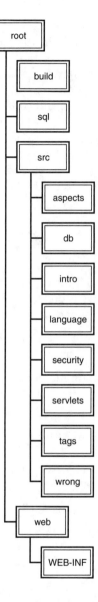

FIGURE 3.2   Project source tree.

Build Process

The build process is performed by Ant and is governed by two files sitting on the top of the source hierarchy: `build.xml` and `build.properties`. The latter contains name-value pairs that indicate, mostly, where things are in the file system. It looks similar to Listing 3.1.

Listing 3.1   `build.properties` File

```
# Subdirectories of the project tree
src=src
build=build
dist=dist
temp=temp
deploy=${catalina}/webapps/${app.name}

# Third party tools
catalina=d:/tools/tomcat-4.0.1
aspectj=d:/t/aspectj1.0
jdbc=d:/tools/mm.mysql.jdbc-1.2c

# Flags and settings
preprocess=false
exclude=aspects/Tracer.java

# How the project is called
app.name=AspectNews
app.version=1.0
```

As you can see, the properties can depend on other properties. The property `deploy`, which denotes the destination directory of the compiled application, depends on where Tomcat is installed (`catalina=d:/tools/tomcat-4.0.1`) and what the application is called (`app.name=AspectNews`). Thus, at runtime this property will be set to `D:/tools/tomcat-4.0.1/webapps/AspectNews`.

The `build.xml` file contains detailed instructions for tools on building the entire project. These instructions are called tasks in Ant's lingo, and the file is presented in Listing 3.2.

LISTING 3.2   `build.xml` File

```
<project name="aj" default="deploy" basedir=".">

  <!-- Set global properties for this build from the file -->
  <property file="build.properties"/>

  <!-- Special task to run AspectJ compiler -->
  <taskdef name="ajc"
```

LISTING 3.2   Continued

```
    classname="org.aspectj.tools.ant.taskdefs.Ajc" >
    <classpath>
      <pathelement location="${aspectj}/aspectj-ant.jar"/>
      <pathelement location="${aspectj}/lib/aspectjtools.jar"/>
    </classpath>
  </taskdef>

  <target name="init"
   description="Do all the preparation work.">
    <!-- Create the build directory structure used by compile -->
    <mkdir dir="${build}"/>
  </target>

  <target name="compile" depends="init"
   description="Creates an executable content in build subdirectory.">

    <!-- Copy the content of the web subdirectory with JSP and configuration files
    to the destination -->
    <copy todir="${build}">
      <fileset dir="web"/>
    </copy>

    <!-- Create subdirectory for classes -->
    <mkdir dir="${build}/WEB-INF/classes"/>

    <!-- Run the AspectJ compiler using the special task -->
    <ajc
      workingdir="${temp}"
      srcdir="${src}"
      preprocess="${preprocess}"
      includes="tags/*,security/*,servlets/*,db/*,aspects/*"
      excludes="${exclude}"
      destdir="${build}/WEB-INF/classes"
    >
      <!-- include libraries needed to compile the target files -->
      <classpath>
        <pathelement location="${aspectj}/lib/aspectjrt.jar"/>
        <pathelement location="${catalina}/common/lib/servlet.jar"/>
      </classpath>
    </ajc>
  </target>
```

LISTING 3.2   Continued

```
<target name="deploy" depends="compile"
 description="Deploy application to servlet container">

  <!-- Copy the contents of the build directory -->
  <mkdir dir="${deploy}"/>
  <copy todir="${deploy}">
    <fileset dir="${build}"/>
  </copy>

  <!-- Copy external dependencies as required -->
  <mkdir  dir="${deploy}/WEB-INF/lib"/>
  <copy
    todir="${deploy}/WEB-INF/lib"
    file="${aspectj}/lib/aspectjrt.jar"
  />
  <copy
    todir="${deploy}/WEB-INF/lib"
    file="${jdbc}/mysql_uncomp.jar"
  />
</target>

</project>
```

Several things in this file deserve special notice. At the beginning, the properties file `build.properties` is read. It is far more convenient to keep properties in a separate file than to edit the main build file every time something changes. Next comes the definition of a special task for AspectJ compiler. Ant comes with a collection of predefined tasks for pretty much anything a reasonable Java developer will need to build a project. But because AspectJ pushes the boundaries, it needs to tell Ant how to run its compiler `ajc`. For that purpose the AspectJ team has developed the special class library that does just that. Ant has to be configured to use it and this is what the task definition task (almost anything in Ant is a task) does—it defines tasks new to Ant, in this case called `ajc` and implemented by the main class `org.aspectj.tools.ant.taskdefs.Ajc`. These two things (reading the property file and defining a special task for `ajc`) are all that is required to configure the build process.

The main content of the build file is the collection of targets. Each target contains a set of tasks that are executed in sequence unless otherwise specified (it will not be in this example). Targets might depend on each other; for example, target `compile` will not execute until target init is done. Target deploy needs to be preceded by compile and so on.

The init target is straightforward, it just creates the build directory. The most interesting target is the compile. First of all, it creates a directory where Java byte codes will go. Second, it executes the AspectJ compilation task ajc. Its attributes correspond to command-line parameters of the AspectJ compiler ajc described in detail in Appendix B, "AspectJ Command-Line Tools" (this is ajc, after all). Their meanings are as follows:

- workingdir is the directory where intermediate files are stored—in this case mapped to the temporary directory. In the case of the preprocess flag set to true (see the following), this is where all precompiled Java files will end up.

- srcdir is the directory where sources are. The particular filenames specified using the includes attribute are relative to this directory.

- preprocess is a flag that tells ajc just to compile aspects to plain Java and stop without producing any byte codes.

- includes lists all the sources that need to be compiled (wild cards are supported). On Listing 3.2 only sources for AspectNews application are specified—packages intro and language are not included into the build process.

- excludes lists all the sources that need not to be compiled (wild cards, again, are supported). It is used to exclude development aspects for production builds.

- destdir specifies where byte codes should go—in this case where the servlet container will expect to find them.

The ajc task also needs the class path. Only two additional libraries are needed: AspectJ's own runtime library aspectjrt.jar and the servlet library from the Tomcat distribution servlet.jar. Note that there is no need for the JDBC library because all needed interfaces are described in the standard java.sql package. The deploy target just copies what has been built in the build directory to Tomcat's Web application hierarchy as specified by the deploy parameter. It also copies two libraries that will be needed at runtime: the AspectJ's runtime and JDBC driver—this time around it is, indeed, needed.

The Ant's build process can be started as follows:

```
shell>ant.bat -file path_to_aj/aj/build.xml target
```

target is the name of the target we are trying to build. If target is omitted, Ant will build the default one—deploy in our example (see Listing 3.2).

Summary

All in all, we have set up our development environment as similar to a generic open source project as possible. It, of course, does not have all the bells and whistles of the source code control-based release process, but it produces a repeatable and configurable sequence of build commands—and this is all that's needed to try the examples that follow.

4

Implementation Details

In this chapter we will discuss the implementation of the example application in its initial state, that is, without any aspects.

Presentation Layer

The presentation layer is implemented using Java Server Pages. Each page described in Table 4.1 contains some presentation functionality plus a statically included header and footer.

TABLE 4.1 JSP Pages

Page	Description
index.jsp	Main page that lists all available pages with their respective functionality.
error.jsp	Error handling page.
login.jsp	Login form.
register.jsp	Registration form.
read.jsp	Page that shows news stories.
select.jsp	Category selection page.
submit.jsp	Page to enter new stories.

The statically included header that follows (header.jsp) contains basic declarations that every page uses:

```
<%@ page errorPage="error.jsp" %>
<%@ page import="java.io.*,java.util.*,db.*" %>
<%@ taglib uri="/tan" prefix="tan" %>
<center>
```

It declares that `error.jsp` will be an error-handling page, imports Java's I/O and utility libraries, and imports AspectNews's library with database access classes. The next statement declares `tan` tag library (`tan` stands for "tags for aspect news," in case you're curious).

The `footer.jsp` just contains a closing center HTML tag and a link to the main page `index.jsp`:

```
<hr>
<p><a href="index.jsp">home</a></p>
</center>
```

These matching `<center>` tags in the static header and footer are all as far as formatting is concerned. The JSPs in the AspectNews application are totally devoid of any decoration for the sake of clarity.

The first major design decision for the AspectNews presentation layer is where the presentation code will reside. The decision is to move as much of the executable code from the JSP as possible, if the application is going to be used with AspectJ.

There is a good reason for the decision: JSPs are compiled "inside" the servlet container at runtime. To do anything useful with JSP and AspectJ you have to trick the servlet container to use `ajc` in place of the regular java compiler, `javac`, or whatever compiler it uses to compile the Java code that is generated from JSP. It is possible, but this option has several big drawbacks:

- There are differences in how both compilers work. For example, `ajc` requires the caller to supply all the files to be compiled with all the names of the compiled pages, which are not known until the JSP is written and installed. So, some rather complex scripts have to be written to discover a full list of files to be compiled.

- The environment that a servlet container uses to compile translated JSPs (that is, libraries, environment variables, compiler settings) varies by container and might not be known at all for non-open source products unless the vendor explicitly provides an interface for customizing the Java compiler.

- A large share of useful pointcuts need class names to work. The names of JSPs get mangled by the servlet container during translation, and the mangling rules also vary by the product, so there is no way to write anything portable based on the JSP name. This all leads to a decision to move any useful code outside JSPs for the AspectNews application, which will only leave formatting HTML tags.

The main page `index.jsp` (Listing 4.1) greets the user and shows the list of available functions (read, submit, select). The username is obtained using the custom tag

<tan:user/>, which gets the user's name from the session attribute user (see Listing 4.2 for the implementation).

LISTING 4.1   index.jsp

```
<html>
<body>
<%@ include file="header.jsp"%>

<h1>Welcome, dear <tan:user /> !</h1>
<p>Please, choose one of the following:<br>
<a href="read.jsp">Read stories</a> stories<br>
<a href="select.jsp">Select</a> topics of interest<br>
<a href="submit.jsp">Submit</a> a story<br>
</p>
<%@ include file="footer.jsp"%>
</body>
</html>
```

LISTING 4.2   UserTag.java

```
package tags;

import java.util.*;
import java.io.*;
import javax.servlet.jsp.*;
import javax.servlet.http.*;
import javax.servlet.jsp.tagext.*;

public class UserTag extends TagSupport
{
    public int doStartTag() throws JspException
    {
        try
        {
            pageContext.getOut().
              print((String)pageContext.getSession().
              getAttribute("user"));
        }
        catch (IOException e)
        {
            throw new JspException("UserTag: " + e.getMessage());
        }
```

LISTING 4.2   Continued

```
        return SKIP_BODY;
    }
    public int doEndTag()
    {
        return EVAL_PAGE;
    }
}
```

How this attribute becomes set is discussed in Chapter 5, "Crosscutting by Design," but for the rest of this chapter it is assumed that it is always there for you to use.

The next pair of JSP and tag combinations (Listing 4.3 and Listing 4.4, respectively) provide the main function of the application: delivery of the stories. The read.jsp page uses the custom <tan:stories/> tag to define a scripting variable text into which the stories are read via the implicit loop defined by StoriesTag.java implementation.

LISTING 4.3   read.jsp

```
<html>
<body>
<%@ include file="header.jsp"%>

<h1>Stories</h1>
<table align=center border=1>
  <tan:stories name="text">
  <tr>
    <td><%=text%></td>
  </tr>
  </tan:stories>
</table>

<%@ include file="footer.jsp"%>

</body>
</html>
```

Exception handling in Listing 4.4 will be discussed in section "Clean Exception Handling" of the next chapter.

LISTING 4.4 StoriesTag.java

```java
package tags;

import java.util.*;
import java.io.*;
import javax.servlet.jsp.*;
import javax.servlet.jsp.tagext.*;
import db.*;

public class StoriesTag extends BodyTagSupport
{
    private String name;
    private Iterator iterator;

    public void setName(String name)
    {
        this.name = name;
    }

    public int doStartTag() throws JspException
    {
        String user = (String)pageContext.getSession().getAttribute("user");
        iterator = StoriesDb.retrieve(user).iterator();

        if(iterator.hasNext())
        {
            Story story = (Story)iterator.next();
            pageContext.setAttribute(name, story.category+" -- "+story.body);
            return EVAL_BODY_TAG;
        }
        else
        {
            return SKIP_BODY;
        }
    }

    public int doAfterBody() throws JspException
    {
        BodyContent body = getBodyContent();

        body.writeOut(getPreviousOut());
```

LISTING 4.4   Continued

```
        body.clearBody();
        if (iterator.hasNext())
        {
            Story story = (Story)iterator.next();
            pageContext.setAttribute(name, story.category+" -- "+story.body);
            return EVAL_BODY_TAG;
        }
        else
        {
            return SKIP_BODY;
        }
    }
}
```

The `StoriesTag.doStartTag()` method retrieves stories for a particular user using `DbStories.retrieve()` method of the database layer (see "Database Operations," later in this section). Stories are represented in objects `Story`, which just bundles individual story text with its respective categories (see Listing 4.5).

LISTING 4.5   `Story.java` Class

```
package db;

public class Story
{
    public String category;
    public String body;

    public Story(String category, String body)
    {
        this.category = category;
        this.body = body;
    }
}
```

Users can select their favorite topics (also known as categories) using the selection page (see Listing 4.6).

LISTING 4.6   `select.jsp`

```
<html>
<body>
<%@ include file="header.jsp"%>

<%!
public static String categories[] =
{
    "POLITICS", "HEALTH", "ENTERTAINMENT",
    "SPORT", "TECHNOLOGY", "BUSINESS"
};
%>
<h1>Preferences for user <tan:user /></h1>

<%
Collection preferences;
if( request.getMethod().equals("POST") )
{
    // Proceess form first
    preferences = new ArrayList();
    for(int i=0; i< categories.length; i++)
    {
        if( null != request.getParameter(categories[i]) )
        {
            preferences.add(categories[i]);
        }
    }
    StoriesDb.savePreferences(
            (String)session.getAttribute("user"), preferences);
}

// Display what was saved
preferences = StoriesDb.preferences(
                        (String)session.getAttribute("user"));
%>

<form method=post action="select.jsp">
<table border=1>
<%
for(int i=0; i< categories.length; i++)
{
```

LISTING 4.6   Continued

```
    String checked = "";
    if( preferences.contains(categories[i]) )
    {
        checked = "checked";
    }
%>
<tr>
    <td><input type=checkbox <%=checked%> name="<%=categories[i]%>"></td>
    <td><%=categories[i]%></td>
</tr>
<%
}
%>
<tr><td colspan=2 align=center>
<input type=submit value="    ok    "></td></tr>
</table>
</form>

<%@ include file="footer.jsp"%>
</body>
</html>
```

This page does not use any custom tags other than `<tan:user/>` and saves and retrieves user's preferences directly with the database layer's methods `StoriesDb.preferences()` method and `StoriesDb.preferencesSave()`. The preferences are held in the page variable `preferences`, which is saved to the database when the page determines that it serves a POST request; that is, the user pressed the OK button on the selection form. The page `submit.jsp` presented on Listing 4.7 works similarly.

LISTING 4.7   submit.jsp

```
<html>
<body>

<%@ include file="header.jsp"%>

<h1>Submit a story</h1>
```

LISTING 4.7   Continued

```
<%
Collection preferences = StoriesDb.preferences(servlets.Util.getUser(session));

if( request.getMethod().equals("POST") )
{
    // Proceess form first
    String category = request.getParameter("category");
    String body     = request.getParameter("body");
    if( null != category && null != body )
    {
        StoriesDb.saveStory(category, body);
    }
}
%>

<form method=post action="submit.jsp">
<textarea name="body" cols="60" rows="10"></textarea><br>
<select name="category">
<%
for(Iterator i=preferences.iterator(); i.hasNext(); )
{
    String category = (String)i.next();
%>
  <option><%=category%></option>
<%
}
%>
</select><br>
<input type=submit value="    ok    ">
</form>

<%@ include file="footer.jsp"%>

</body>
</html>
```

This concludes the description of the presentation layer of the AspectNews application. Pages login.jsp, register.jsp, and error.jsp will be discussed in Chapter 5.

Configuration and Initialization

Because AspectNews is a Web application, the natural way to configure it would be to use the application deployment descriptor (see Listing 4.8). This is an XML file to which servlets will have guaranteed access at runtime (strictly speaking, servlets do not need direct access to the file itself, but an API to get to its content is available). It compares favorably to some other plain text configuration file, or even a JNDI accessible repository, because it becomes part of the application execution context and as such, no additional bootstrapping is needed. The only possible objection is the XML syntax—it is a definite overkill for simple name-value pairs. But, as any design decision, it is a compromise—some like it hot and nobody's perfect.

LISTING 4.8   Application Deployment Descriptor `web.xml`

```
<!DOCTYPE web-app
    PUBLIC "-//Sun Microsystems, Inc.//DTD Web Application 2.3//EN"
    "http://java.sun.com/dtd/web-app_2_3.dtd">

<web-app>

    <!-- General description of your web application -->

    <display-name>Aspect News</display-name>
    <description>
      This is version 1.0 of an application to perform news reading
      and publishing, based on servlets, aspects and JSP pages.
    </description>

    <context-param>
      <param-name>dbdriver</param-name>
      <param-value>org.gjt.mm.mysql.Driver</param-value>
      <description>The database driver class.</description>
    </context-param>

    <context-param>
      <param-name>dburl</param-name>
      <param-value>jdbc:mysql://localhost/an</param-value>
      <description>The database connecting URL.</description>
    </context-param>

    <context-param>
      <param-name>dbuser</param-name>
      <param-value>scott</param-value>
```

LISTING 4.8   Continued

```xml
      <description>The database log-in.</description>
  </context-param>

  <context-param>
    <param-name>dbpass</param-name>
    <param-value>tiger</param-value>
    <description>The database password.</description>
  </context-param>

  <servlet>
    <servlet-name>register</servlet-name>
    <description>
      This servlet registers users. It processes requests
      from the register.jsp page.
    </description>
    <servlet-class>servlets.Register</servlet-class>
    <load-on-startup>2</load-on-startup>
  </servlet>

  <servlet>
    <servlet-name>init</servlet-name>
    <description>
      This servlet holds initialization parameters and the context.
    </description>
    <servlet-class>servlets.Init</servlet-class>
    <load-on-startup>1</load-on-startup>
  </servlet>

  <servlet-mapping>
    <servlet-name>register</servlet-name>
    <url-pattern>/register</url-pattern>
  </servlet-mapping>


  <!-- Define the default session timeout for your application,
       in minutes
  -->
  <session-config>
    <session-timeout>30</session-timeout>    <!-- 30 minutes -->
  </session-config>
```

LISTING 4.8   Continued

```
    <taglib>
        <taglib-uri>
            /tan
        </taglib-uri>
        <taglib-location>
            /WEB-INF/tan.tld
        </taglib-location>
    </taglib>
</web-app>
```

The file needs to exist anyway because it is required to do so, and because it contains servlets' declarations, mappings, and the declaration of our tag library. The servlet declaration section of the file just declares mapping between servlet name and its implementation class. The servlet mapping section tells the container what is the URL that invokes a given servlet. The `<taglib>` element instructs the servlet container that there is a tag library in the application that will be accessed by the name "tan" and its configuration file is in an XML file called `tan.tld` (see Listing 4.9).

LISTING 4.9   Tag Library Descriptor `tan.tld`

```
<?xml version="1.0" encoding="ISO-8859-1" ?>
<!DOCTYPE taglib
    PUBLIC "-//Sun Microsystems, Inc.//DTD JSP Tag Library 1.1//EN"
        "http://java.sun.com/j2ee/dtds/web-jsptaglibrary_1_1.dtd">

<taglib>

    <tlibversion>1.0</tlibversion>
    <jspversion>1.1</jspversion>
    <shortname></shortname>

    <tag>
        <name>user</name>
        <tagclass>tags.UserTag</tagclass>
        <bodycontent>empty</bodycontent>
    </tag>

    <tag>
        <name>stories</name>
        <tagclass>tags.StoriesTag</tagclass>
```

LISTING 4.9   Continued

```
    <teiclass>tags.StoriesEI</teiclass>
    <bodycontent>JSP</bodycontent>
    <info>
        A tag that prints stories.
    </info>
    <attribute>
      <name>name</name>
      <required>true</required>
      <rtexprvalue>true</rtexprvalue>
    </attribute>
  </tag>

</taglib>
```

The tag library descriptor defines the tags used in the JSP pages (see the
"Presentation Layer" section in this chapter) and ties them to classes that implement
their (tags) functionality.

Now back to configuration and initialization. What does the application need from
its environment? First, it needs name-value pairs from the deployment descriptor
(see Listing 4.8) that will tell it how to connect to the database. Second, it needs to
be told how to log messages to the error log. Message logging won't be discussed
until Chapter 6, "Development Aids," but the conduit for the messages must be
provided. Because both things (configuration parameters and logging functionality)
are available for servlets and your goal is to provide the same for any part of the
application, you will write a rather unusual servlet that will provide needed interfaces (see Listing 4.10).

LISTING 4.10   Init.java Servlet

```
package servlets;

import java.util.*;
import javax.servlet.*;
import javax.servlet.http.*;

public class Init extends HttpServlet
{
    private static ServletContext sc = null;

    public static String getParameter(String key)
    {
```

LISTING 4.10   Continued

```
            return sc.getInitParameter(key);
    }

    public static void log(String message)
    {
        sc.log(message);
    }

    public static void log(String message, Throwable throwable)
    {
        sc.log(message, throwable);
    }

    public void init() throws ServletException
    {
        sc = getServletContext();

        try
        {
            Class.forName(getParameter("dbdriver")).newInstance();
        }
        catch(Exception e)
        {
            throw new ServletException("Cannot load JDBC driver :"+
                getParameter("dbdriver"), e);
        }
    }
}
```

The unusual thing about this listing is that besides all the access methods, it doesn't implement anything that makes servlet a servlet—no doPost(), doGet(), or service() methods are implemented. From the whole servlet interface the only realized method is init(), which is the servlet's purpose: to be loaded on startup and provide interfaces to the inner content of the servlet container via static variable sc of type ServletContext. To be on the safe side, no URL is configured to be used to access the servlet (see Listing 4.8; there is no <servlet-mapping> element for it) because there is no reason to access it.

As an added bonus, the init() method also loads a JDBC driver according to the class name specified in the configuration parameter dbdriver.

Database Operations

In AspectNews application database operations occur in several packages: db, servlets, and security. The class db.StoriesDb (see Listing 4.11) implements all the persistence needed for the application's business logic.

LISTING 4.11   StoriesDb.java

```java
package db;

import java.sql.*;
import java.util.*;
import servlets.Init;

public class StoriesDb
{
    public static Collection retrieve(String user) throws Exception
    {
        Collection res = new ArrayList();

        Connection conn = DriverManager.getConnection(
            Init.getParameter("dburl"),
            Init.getParameter("dbuser"),
            Init.getParameter("dbpass"));
        Statement stmt = conn.createStatement();

        ResultSet rs = stmt.executeQuery(
          "SELECT stories.category, stories.body "+
          "FROM stories, preferences WHERE preferences.name='"+user+
          "' AND stories.category=preferences.category");

        while (rs.next())
        {
            res.add(new Story(rs.getString(1), rs.getString(2)));
        }

        conn.close();
        return res;
    }

    public static Collection preferences(String user) throws Exception
    {
        Collection res = new ArrayList();
```

LISTING 4.11   Continued

```
        Connection conn = DriverManager.getConnection(
            Init.getParameter("dburl"),
            Init.getParameter("dbuser"),
            Init.getParameter("dbpass"));
        Statement stmt = conn.createStatement();

        ResultSet rs = stmt.executeQuery(
          "SELECT category FROM preferences WHERE name='"+user+"'");

        while (rs.next())
        {
            res.add(rs.getString(1));
        }

        conn.close();
        return res;
    }

    public static void savePreferences(String user, Collection preferences)
      throws Exception
    {
        Connection conn = DriverManager.getConnection(
            Init.getParameter("dburl"),
            Init.getParameter("dbuser"),
            Init.getParameter("dbpass"));
        Statement stmt = conn.createStatement();

        stmt.executeUpdate("DELETE FROM preferences WHERE name='"+user+"'");

        Iterator iterator = preferences.iterator();
        while(iterator.hasNext())
        {
            stmt.executeUpdate(
              "INSERT INTO preferences (name, category) VALUES('"+
              user+"', '"+(String)iterator.next()+"')");
        }

        conn.close();
    }
```

LISTING 4.11   Continued

```
public static void saveStory(String category, String body) throws Exception
{
    Connection conn = DriverManager.getConnection(
        Init.getParameter("dburl"),
        Init.getParameter("dbuser"),
        Init.getParameter("dbpass"));
    Statement stmt = conn.createStatement();

    stmt.executeUpdate("INSERT INTO stories (category, body) VALUES('"+
        category+"', '"+body+"')");

    conn.close();
}
}
```

Database connectivity parameters are obtained from the Init servlet. Please note, that database-related code in this application does not check for SQL strings to be properly formatted; for example, a presence of a single quote character (') will cause an SQLException to be thrown. It is easy to fix, but this functionality is left out for two reasons: to keep examples shorter and to be able to break the application at will to test the exception handling mechanism, which is discussed in Chapter 5.

Database operations in servlets and security packages are also discussed in Chapter 5.

Summary

This concludes the description of the AspectNews application—it is compact enough to fit into about a dozen source files, yet it is sufficiently complex to illustrate the concepts of aspect-oriented programming in action.

So far, there was no word on aspects in the implementation of this application. In the next chapter, we will start introducing them as the application starts taking shape.

5

Crosscutting by Design

So far, the AspectNews application has managed just fine without aspects. In this chapter we will start introducing aspects to its structure to improve on the application's design.

AspectNews would function as currently written (albeit insecure) with the exception that it would not know the identity of the user (this is perhaps the ultimate security: no user—no data). This illustrates an important point: Some aspects can be optional and some will be embedded into the application design. By the word *optional* I mean that the functionality represented by such an aspect can be included or excluded from the finished application at will without affecting its business utility, meaning these aspects can be used as development aids. The aspects of embedded kind represent design decisions, which implement certain chunks of the application as crosscutting concerns, and they become inalienable modules of the finished production system.

The decision to address the security concerns as an aspect belongs to the embedded category—the application will not function without it. Although aspects created as development aids are undeniably useful, the true economic benefit of the whole aspect-oriented programming concept lays in the increased modularity of the overall design—the production aspects that unload repeating, boring, and wasteful functionality that would otherwise pollute the core business logic code. In real life, of course, the boundary between development and production aspects can quickly become blurred and what was meant as a development nicety eventually becomes an integral part of the system. (Ever heard of scope creep?)

Security

Security is the first truly crosscutting concern of the AspectNews application. The goal of the security subsystem is to prohibit page access for unauthenticated users. There are several ways to do this:

- Use security facilities of the frontend Web server (Internet Information Server, Apache, iPlanet, and so on) that connects to the servlet engine.

- Use the authentication feature of the servlet container if it is implemented (it should be if the container is compliant with v.2.3 of the servlet specification. See Appendix F, "References").

- Implement a security subsystem from scratch.

Naturally, we choose the last option because it allows for most flexibility in functionality and is most suitable for illustration purposes.

The security subsystem workflow will roughly follow the servlet's form-based specification (see Figure 5.1):

1. A user will try to access a JSP page.

2. If the user was not authenticated or the authentication has expired, the login form will be presented.

3. The user submits his ID and passwords and if they are deemed valid gets redirected to the Startup page of the application.

Any user can register himself with the application, thus gaining access to its functionality.

Security Exception and Its Handling

Because it is a Web application, the natural place to store authentication information is a session. The fact that a user has been successfully authenticated will be reflected by a session attribute called user, which will contain the user ID. To work, the security subsystem has to check on the presence of the user attribute constantly and transparently.

Let's start with transparency. It means that the security concern should be addressed as unobtrusive to the core application logic as possible. One of the ways to achieve this is to implement security signaling by utilizing a natural way for a JSP page to handle exceptions, that is, by introducing a new security exception class that extends the JspException (see Listing 5.1).

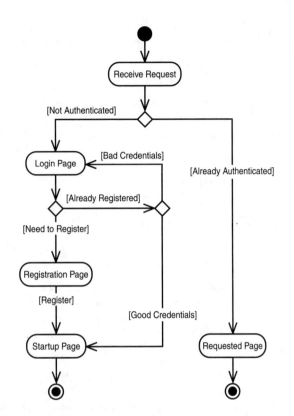

FIGURE 5.1   Security activity diagram.

LISTING 5.1   NotAuthenticated.java Exception

```
package security;

import javax.servlet.jsp.*;

public class NotAuthenticated extends JspException
{
    NotAuthenticated()
    {
        super();
    }

    NotAuthenticated(String msg)
    {
```

LISTING 5.1   Continued

```
        super(msg);
    }

    NotAuthenticated(String msg, Throwable rootCause)
    {
        super(msg, rootCause);
    }

    NotAuthenticated(Throwable rootCause)
    {
        super(rootCause);
    }
}
```

For all participants of the JSP game the NotAuthenticated exception will be treated as a JspException(because it is)—until the security subsystem will be ready to deal with it. As was described in Chapter 4, the error handler for all the JSP pages in the application is a page called error.jsp (see the section entitled "Clean Exception Handling").

All exceptions thrown during the JSP processing will end up in this page—including NotAuthenticated. The only thing for the error page to do is to look for it and, if received, forward the request to the login page (see Listing 5.2) where the user will have a chance to redeem himself with proper credentials.

LISTING 5.2   login.jsp

```
<html>
<body>
<%@ include file="header.jsp"%>

<h1>Please, log in!</h1>

<form method=post action="index.jsp">
User: <input type=text name="user"><br>
Password:<input type=password name="pass"><br>
<input type=submit value="    ok    ">
</form>
<p>New users: please <a href="register.jsp">register</a> yourselves.</p>
```

LISTING 5.2   Continued

```
<%@ include file="footer.jsp"%>
</body>
</html>
```

Proactive Security Verification

So far, the handling of the security violation was transparent for the core application. But what about checking? Unfortunately, only semitransparency can be achieved. Because the only reliable holder of the security context is the session (ultimately, it goes down to a cookie with the session ID that a browser sends with every request), the security subsystem—no matter how implemented—has to have an access to it. This is the *semi* part of the semitransparency, meaning, something has to happen that exposes the session to the security subsystem. The *transparent* part of semitransparency is that this can be made automatic if some basic operation involves the session.

The good news is all classes that implement custom JSP tags have access to the user's session. Thus, theoretically, if a page uses any custom tags, it can be made uniformly secure by creating a pointcut that picks all calls to doStartTag() methods, and some smart advice will run verifying credentials. Ideally, the advice would look like the one presented in Listing 5.3. Note the usage of the anonymous pointcut syntax: The pointcut call(int *.doStartTag()) is defined directly after the advice declaration and does not have a name—sometimes this notation makes aspects more readable.

LISTING 5.3   Ideal Security Advice

```
int around() throws JspException: call(int *.doStartTag())
{
  TagSupport ts = (TagSupport)thisJoinPoint.getTarget();
  PageContext pc = ts.getPageContext();
  String user = (String)pc.getSession().getAttribute("user");
  if( null == user )
  {
    throw new NotAuthenticated();
  }

  return proceed();
}
```

Unfortunately, there are two complications. First, what if a page does not use any custom tags? For example, submit.jsp shown in Listing 4.7 does not show anything produced by the tag library, it just needs the user ID. Luckily, it uses one of the utility methods (see Listing 5.4) that can be advised by an aspect.

LISTING 5.4   `Util.java` Class

```
package servlets;

import javax.servlet.http.*;

public class Util
{
    public static String getUser(HttpSession sess) throws Exception
    {
        return (String)sess.getAttribute("user");
    }
}
```

But what if a similar page does not call the utility method `getUser()`, if it calls `session.getAttribute("user")` directly? Then a runtime error would occur if no user attribute could be found. It would not be a security breach because this attribute can be set only after proper authentication. Nevertheless, this illustrates a very important point: The security context (a session in this case) has to be implicitly or explicitly exposed to the security concern, or, more generally, the join points have to be accessible in order for the aspects to do their job. To somewhat alleviate the issue, you must develop as many pointcuts and advices as needed to cover all possible security checking wherever the session context is exposed to it, at least for all methods that receive a session parameter.

The second complication is a purely technical one: The `pageContext` variable in the `javax.servlet.jsp.tagext.TagSupport` class is protected; that is, it cannot be accessed as shown in Listing 5.3. The solution is to create a pair of intermediary classes (one for `TagSupport` and another one for `BodyTagSupport`) that make this variable somehow accessible (see Figure 5.2).

Listing 5.5 shows an example of such a class. (`security.BodyTagSupport` Class is similar).

LISTING 5.5   `security.tagSupport` Class

```
package security;

import javax.servlet.jsp.*;

class TagSupport extends javax.servlet.jsp.tagext.TagSupport
{
```

LISTING 5.5   Continued

```
public TagSupport()
{
    super();
}

public PageContext getPageContext()
{
    return pageContext;
}
}
```

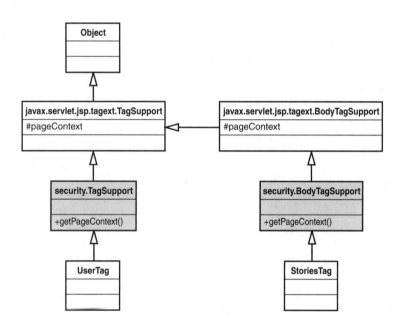

FIGURE 5.2   Exposing the page context in tag support hierarchy.

The only claim to fame of these two classes is their method getPageContext(), which provides much needed access to the page's and, in turn, the servlet's execution context to whoever will be calling. One straightforward solution to get these classes into the object hierarchy is to have UserTag (see Listing 4.2) and StoriesTag (see Listing 4.4) extend them instead of javax.servlet.jsp.tagext.TagSupport and javax.servlet.jsp.tagext. BodyTagSupport, respectively. That, however, would be a dead giveaway of the security subsystem to the rest of the application.

Putting It All into an Aspect

AspectJ has a feature called *static crosscutting* that addresses this problem. In practical terms, it means that an aspect can change the static class hierarchy by introducing an interface or a parent class for an existing class. It allows us to leave package tags untouched (in the source code meaning of the word) and change its classes' parents to make it convenient (or, more precisely, possible) for the security aspect to access the page context. The resulting aspect is presented in Listing 5.6 and is a good illustration that reality bites—it is a long way from the originally elegant concept presented in Listing 5.3.

LISTING 5.6   `Authentication.java` Aspect

```
package security;

import javax.servlet.*;
import javax.servlet.http.*;
import javax.servlet.jsp.*;
import tags.*;
public aspect Authentication
{
    declare parents: UserTag extends TagSupport;
    declare parents: StoriesTag extends BodyTagSupport;

    pointcut startTag():
       call(int *.doStartTag())
       &&
       (target(TagSupport) || target(BodyTagSupport));

    pointcut sessionParam(HttpSession sess):
       call(* *.*(.., HttpSession, ..)) && args(sess);

    int around() throws JspException: startTag()
    {
       PageContext pc;
       Object o = thisJoinPoint.getTarget();
       if(o instanceof TagSupport)
       {
           pc = ((TagSupport)o).getPageContext();
       }
       else if(o instanceof BodyTagSupport)
       {
           pc = ((BodyTagSupport)o).getPageContext();
       }
```

LISTING 5.6   Continued

```
        else
        {
            throw new JspException(
                "Unknown target class: "+o.getClass().getName());
        }

        String user = (String)pc.getSession().getAttribute("user");

        if( null == user )
        {
            ServletRequest req = pc.getRequest();
            user = req.getParameter("user");
            String pass = req.getParameter("pass");
            if( (null == user) || (null == pass) )
            {
                throw new NotAuthenticated();
            }

            try
            {
                if( !UsersDb.check(user, pass) )
                {
                    pc.getServletConfig().
                        getServletContext().
                        getRequestDispatcher("/login.jsp").
                        forward(req, pc.getResponse());

                    return javax.servlet.jsp.tagext.Tag.SKIP_BODY;
                }
            }
            catch(Exception e)
            {
                throw new JspException(e);
            }

            pc.getSession().setAttribute("user", user);
        }

        return proceed();
    }
```

LISTING 5.6   Continued

```
    before(HttpSession sess) throws JspException: sessionParam(sess)
    {
        if( null == sess.getAttribute("user") )
        {
            throw new NotAuthenticated();
        }
    }
}
```

The first two statements of the aspect introduce UserTag and StoriesTag classes to their new parents (by the way, an *introduction* is the official name of the AspectJ operation used here). Because the Authentication aspect is totally oblivious to the javax.servlet.jsp.tagext package, the TagSupport and BodyTagSupport classes referred to here do belong to the current package security. By the virtue of this operation, our tag classes' hierarchies were changed without detection, as depicted in Figure 5.2.

The first pointcut, startTag(), got a little bit more complicated than was originally intended. It comprises several primitive pointcuts tied in a logical expression. First, call(int *.doStartTag()) picks all calls to methods named doStartTag() returning int regardless of their object association. A problem exists here because the regular (not augmented) javax.servlet.jsp.tagext.TagSupport class is pretty useless for your purposes, you cannot just start picking doStartTag() calls of all javax.servlet.jsp.tagext.TagSupports subclasses. (If you could, the syntax for such a pointcut would have been call(int javax.servlet.jsp.tagext.TagSupport+.doStartTag()), meaning "methods doStartTag() of TagSupport and its subclasses"). The * symbol in the pointcut means "all classes," and the real problem is that the pointcut might pick something that has nothing to do with our newly introduced classes that expose the page context.

The second part of the startTag() pointcut explicitly instructs it to pick only targets that extend to either security.TagSupport or security.BodyTagSupport. The around() advice executes when the startTag() pointcut picks its join points, as described earlier. The first order of business is to get the page context. The getTarget() method of the current join point returns the currently executing target object; in this case, the object on which doStartTag() method would be called (if not for the advice that is). The series of if-else statements tries to determine the exact type of the target object. Strictly speaking, the last else is not needed because the startTag() pointcut picks either security.TagSupport or security.BodyTagSupport. But things do get changed and nobody knows how this advice will be utilized in the future (that is, with what pointcuts), so it is better to throw a meaningful exception now than get a runtime illegal cast error later.

After the page context is successfully obtained, it is a matter of trivial coding to implement the logic shown in Figure 5.2. If the user has been authenticated already, the advice leaves everybody alone and proceed()s (pun intended). If not, there are two possibilities:

- The user requested a page. In this case, the exception NotAuthenticated is thrown. As discussed before, it will be handled by the error page, which will forward the request to the login page.

- The user completed the login information in the login page (see Listing 5.2), and his credentials need to be checked. This is done by the database method UsersDb.check() (see Listing 5.7) and if results are not satisfactory, the request gets forwarded to the login page. At this point we cannot just throw another NotAuthenticated exception because the error page's context has already ceased to exist. This is also the reason that it has to be an around() advice instead of before()—the execution flow is decisively interrupted, and the original call to get a custom tag value never gets fulfilled until valid credentials are provided. But if they are, the session attribute gets set, and the execution flow continues to the proceed() pseudo-call.

LISTING 5.7   UsersDb.java

```
package security;

import java.io.*;
import java.util.*;
import java.sql.*;
import servlets.Init;

public class UsersDb
{
    public static boolean check(String user, String pass) throws Exception
    {
        String dbPass = "";

        Connection conn = DriverManager.getConnection(
            Init.getParameter("dburl"),
            Init.getParameter("dbuser"),
            Init.getParameter("dbpass"));
        Statement stmt = conn.createStatement();
```

LISTING 5.7   Continued

```
    ResultSet rs =
     stmt.executeQuery("SELECT pass FROM users WHERE name='"+user+"'");

    if(rs.next())
    {
        dbPass = rs.getString(1);
    }

    conn.close();

    if( dbPass.equals(pass) )
    {
        return true;
    }

    return false;
  }
   }
```

The intent for the second pointcut, sessionParam(HttpSession), is primarily to pick calls to the servlets.Util.getUser() (see Listing 5.4) method to verify that the user has been authenticated. While you're at it, you also can write a very general pointcut that will pick all methods that receive a parameter of type javax.servlet.http.HttpSession. It means that you are going to protect any method that has anything to do with a session from unauthorized user's access.

Here are the details:

- The sessionParam(HttpSession) pointcut has a parameter, which is exposed for the consequent use in the advice by the primitive pointcut args(). The latter picks all join points where types of the arguments match the types listed.

- The .. pattern sign in the method signature means "any number of arguments of any types."

- The type pattern * *.* means "any method of any class returning anything." The before(HttpSession) advice receives the parameter exposed by the sessionParam(HttpSession) pointcut and uses it to check on the "user" attribute. This is the extent of what it can do because no other interesting parts of the request execution context are available to it.

Registration

The registration page (see Listing 5.8) uses the registration servlet as its action (see Listing 5.9). The servlet simply saves whatever information was received from the registration form and authenticates the user.

LISTING 5.8 `register.jsp`

```
<html>
<body>
<%@ include file="header.jsp"%>

<h1>Please, register yourself!</h1>

<form method=post action="register">
User: <input type=text name="user"><br>
Password:<input type=password name="pass"><br>
<input type=submit value="    register    ">
</form>

<%@ include file="footer.jsp"%>

</body>
</html>
```

After authenticating (which is just setting the `"user"` attribute in the session) the request is redirected to the start up page.

LISTING 5.9 `Register.java` Servlet

```
package servlets;

import javax.servlet.*;
import javax.servlet.http.*;
import java.sql.*;

public class Register extends HttpServlet
{
    public void doPost(HttpServletRequest request,
        HttpServletResponse response) throws ServletException
    {
        try
        {
```

LISTING 5.9   Continued

```
        String user = (String) request.getParameter("user");
        String pass = (String) request.getParameter("pass");

        Connection conn = DriverManager.getConnection(
            Init.getParameter("dburl"),
            Init.getParameter("dbuser"),
            Init.getParameter("dbpass"));
        conn.createStatement().executeUpdate(
            "INSERT INTO users (name, pass) VALUES('"+user+"','"
            +pass+"')");
        conn.close();

        request.getSession(true).setAttribute("user", user);
        log("Registered user '"+user+"'");

        response.sendRedirect("index.jsp");
        return;
    }
    catch(Exception e)
    {
        throw new ServletException(e);
    }
  }
}
```

Design by Contract and Other Coding Improvements

One of the most powerful ideas in object-oriented programming (and in computer science in general) is a design by the contract. It was fully developed by Bertrand Meyer (see Appendix F, "References" for more information) and, in a nutshell, states that various methods, by executing themselves properly, must fulfill their explicit contract that can be verified. Some programming languages have built-in facilities for contract verification; Java does not, however, but assertions are coming (see Appendix F). The trivial solution for so-called precondition verification is to insert some code at the beginning of each method that ensures certain conditions are met before a method begins executing. It is quite laborious, which presents a perfect case for AspectJ to show its strengths.

The AspectNews application has a particular troublesome area in its db package. An implicit contract of all the database methods is to receive parameters that are not nulls. As you saw in Listing 4.11, no explicit precautions are taken to prevent this from happening. Fortunately, aspects can provide a clean and crosscutting solution to the problem (see Listing 5.10).

LISTING 5.10　NullChecker.java Aspect

```
package aspects;

public aspect NullChecker
{
    pointcut arguments(): execution(* db.*.*(..));

    before() : arguments()
    {
        Object args[] = thisJoinPoint.getArgs();
        for(int i=0; i<args.length; i++)
        {
            if( null == args[i] )
            {
                throw new
                    IllegalArgumentException("The argument is null.");
            }
        }
    }
}
```

The arguments() pointcut picks an execution of all database methods in the db package. When the before() advice executes, it obtains this join point's arguments (in this case the target methods' arguments) using getArgs() introspection API call. The arguments then compared to null one by one and if a null is found, a runtime exception IllegalArgumentException is thrown. Because it is a runtime exception, no additional declarations are required. Because the before() advice will be executing before target's method body, it is guaranteed that no nulls will ever reach the database layer of code.

A similar effect can be achieved using assertions introduced in Java v.1.4. The assertions, however, are not best suited for contract enforcement. First of all, they can be disabled at runtime, and, second, they do not throw meaningful exceptions. Most importantly, assertions do not have any crosscutting properties; they have to be purposefully and manually coded. The contract enforcing aspects, on the other hand, can uniformly apply arbitrary complex contract policy throughout the system.

The post-condition checking can be constructed similarly using the after() advices.

Good design techniques can also be enforced using AspectJ static crosscutting. Consider the following problem and the solution offered by AspectJ. The AspectNews application has database code throughout. In this case, it is done on purpose to illustrate various forms of crosscutting, but, generally, it is a bad idea. The code will be more maintainable if segregated along the functional lines. Coincidentally, modularization is one of the goals of aspect-oriented programming. To achieve this goal, one can use the AspectJ compiler's capability to check on static pointcuts. The compiler can generate warnings and errors when a pointcut is reached (see Listing 5.11).

LISTING 5.11   CodeSegregation.java Aspect

```
package aspects;

import java.sql.*;

public aspect CodeSegregation
{
    pointcut dbCode()     :
                        call(Connection DriverManager.getConnection(..));
    pointcut badDbCode() :
                        dbCode() && !within(db.*);
    pointcut reallyBadDbCode():
            badDbCode() && !within(security.*) && !within(servlets.*);

    declare warning: badDbCode()     :
                                "Database code outside 'db' package.";
    declare error   : reallyBadDbCode():
                                "Database code here is not permitted.";
}
```

Let's say that our goal is to prevent developers from coding low-level database operations outside the db package. The pointcut dbCode() can detect such things by picking calls to getConnection() method—a cornerstone of the JDBC API. Armed with this pointcut, the next pointcut, badDbCode(), will pick all such calls made outside db package. A warning is issued if such usage will be discovered during compilation. In the case of AspectNews this declaration produces something like this:

```
...\src\security\UsersDb.java:31:27: Database code outside 'db' package. (warning)
        Connection conn = DriverManager.getConnection(
                      ^

...\src\servlets\Register.java:41:31: Database code outside 'db' package. (warning)
            Connection conn = DriverManager.getConnection(
                      ^
```

The aspect correctly discovered that the database code is also located in `security.UsersDb` and `servlets.Register` classes. Because this message declared only as a warning, the compilation will continue and complete successfully.

The next pointcut, `reallyBadDbCode()`, uses `badDbCode()` (meaning `getConnection()` calls outside the `db` package) and adds to it exclusions of security and servlets packages where database code will be tolerated. The error declaration based on the `reallyBadDbCode()` pointcut instructs the compiler to complain and stop if any of the join points picked by this pointcut can ever be reached. This will stop any attempts to put a database code anywhere but into the `db` package and all such attempts in security or servlets packages will be flagged.

Clean Exception Handling

One of the most important characteristics of the well-behaved application is its capability to recover from errors or, in Java-speak, to handle exceptions gracefully. In a distributed application it is somewhat more complicated because some errors should be propagated to the end users, some ignored, from some the application can recover transparently, and so on. For a typical Java application the exception handling logic can easily take up to 30% of all code.

In the case of AspectNews we can select a simplified exception handling policy, which states that all exceptions should be handled by notifying the end user that something went wrong and providing all the gory details in the application log file. Your only concern will be cleaning up the code from unnecessary try-catch blocks— and, yes, this can be qualified as truly crosscutting concern by anyone who has ever developed a Java application with more than a dozen classes.

Let's consider the `StoriesDb` class again (see Listing 4.11). This class uses a lot of JDBC API calls that throw `SQLExceptions`, which are declared in the methods' signatures. Yet, the `StoriesTag` class (see Listing 4.4) does not seem to care. Compare the "proper" version of this class (see Listing 5.12) with what is actually implemented (see Listing 4.4).

LISTING 5.12   `StoriesTag.java` Class Again, Now in the "Proper" Form

```
package tags;

import java.util.*;
import java.io.*;
import javax.servlet.jsp.*;
import javax.servlet.jsp.tagext.*;
import db.*;
```

LISTING 5.12 Continued

```java
public class StoriesTag extends BodyTagSupport
{
    private String name;
    private Iterator iterator;

    public void setName(String name)
    {
      this.name = name;
    }

    public int doStartTag() throws JspException
    {
      try
      {
        String user = (String)pageContext.getSession().
          getAttribute("user");
        iterator = StoriesDb.retrieve(user).iterator();

        if(iterator.hasNext())
        {
          Story story =
            (Story)iterator.next();
          pageContext.setAttribute(name, story.category+" -- "+
            story.body);
          return EVAL_BODY_TAG;
        }
        else
        {
          return SKIP_BODY;
        }
      }
      catch(Throwable e)
      {
        throw new JspException(e);
      }
    }

    public int doAfterBody() throws JspException
    {
      BodyContent body = getBodyContent();
```

LISTING 5.12   Continued

```
      try
      {
        body.writeOut(getPreviousOut());
      }
      catch (IOException e)
      {
        throw new JspTagException("IterationTag: "+e.getMessage());
      }

      body.clearBody();
      if (iterator.hasNext())
      {
        Story story =(Story)iterator.next();
        pageContext.setAttribute(name, story.category+
          " -- "+story.body);
        return EVAL_BODY_TAG;
      }
      else
      {
        return SKIP_BODY;
      }
    }
}
```

The proper form of the class contains all the needed exception handling code:
StoriesDb.retrieve() throws SQLException and BodyContent.writeOut() throws
IOException. Diligent programmers have to recast both as JspTagException because
this is the only thing that can possibly be thrown out of tag classes, as mandated by
the JSP API. This operation, in effect, wraps the original exception into something
that the JSP layer can handle, thus loosing the original exception typing information. That is, if there will be any handling logic based on exception type, this is the
last chance to use it otherwise it will be wrapped forever.

From the other side, the typing information presents one problem of its own: It has
to be recognized. In the previous example, the exception to be handled is of type
SQLException. Strictly speaking, the presentation layer should not care what kind of
repository is used to keep the stories. Catching the mother of them all
(java.lang.Throwable) is an attempt to disassociate the repository type (in this case,
a SQL database) from the presentation and, generally, hide the flow-breaking exceptions forever—until handled by our code that is. In other words, the type information becomes hidden again—this time on purpose.

The AspectJ's value proposition for this problem is simple and elegant: If an exception type is of no particular importance, it can be automatically wrapped into a subclass of `RuntimeException`, so no additional code will be required until it reaches its ultimate destination. The aspect that allows this to happen for the `StoriesTag` class (see Listing 4.4) is shown on Listing 5.13.

LISTING 5.13   Exceptions.java Aspect

```
package aspects;

import java.sql.*;
import java.io.*;
import javax.servlet.jsp.tagext.*;

public aspect Exceptions
{
    declare soft : SQLException : call(* db.StoriesDb.*(..));
    declare soft : IOException  : call(* BodyContent.writeOut(..));
}
```

This aspect instructs the AspectJ compiler to "soften" exceptions mentioned in the declaration if they are thrown at the join points specified by the pointcut that follows. The "softening" means wrapping the original exception in `org.aspectj.lang.SoftException` in a way similar to the way the `javax.servletServletException` does it; the difference is that AspectJ compiler does it automatically and consistently. The original exception can be later retrieved using `SoftException.getWrappedThrowable()` API method.

The first declaration affects all the calls made to methods of `db.StoriesDb` class in all advisable code of the AspectNews application. Another way to achieve the same thing would be to declare

```
declare soft : SQLException : execution(* db.StoriesDb.*(..));
```

It would have shut down (or "soften") the `SQLException` right inside of the `StoriesDb` class, and its methods could be written without even declaring the fact that they throw it. This approach is, probably, less clean because some other application would not be able to utilize this class without the `Exceptions` aspect attached to it. The version presented on Listing 5.14 makes softening more explicit.

The second declaration softens the `IOException` of one of the JSP utility methods. This exception is an even better candidate for softening because an application developer does not have any control whatsoever of what this method is doing and when this exception can be thrown—in all likelihood, it would indicate some serious error inside the servlet container. Handling these kinds of exceptions inside presentation code will not add anything to the application's usefulness.

The discussion of the error-handling page of this application was postponed several times throughout previous chapters. At this point, all pieces of the puzzle have fallen into the place and Listing 5.14 shows it in all its glory.

LISTING 5.14   error.jsp

```
<html>
<body>

<%@ page isErrorPage="true" %>
<%@ page import="java.io.*,java.util.*,security.*" %>

<%
String message = exception.getMessage();

if(exception instanceof NotAuthenticated)
{
%>
   <jsp:forward page="login.jsp"/>
<%
}

log("Got exception", exception);
if(exception instanceof javax.servlet.jsp.JspException)
{
    log("Root cause for JspException",
          ((javax.servlet.jsp.JspException)exception).getRootCause());
    message = "System Error.";
}

if(exception instanceof org.aspectj.lang.SoftException)
{
    log("Wrapped in SoftException",
    ((org.aspectj.lang.SoftException)exception).getWrappedThrowable());
    message = "System Error.";
}

if(exception instanceof java.sql.SQLException)
{
    message = "Database Error.";
```

LISTING 5.14   Continued

```
}
%>

<h1 align=center>Sorry!</h1>
<p align=center>Got a problem: <%=message%></p>

</body>
</html>
```

Overall, Listing 5.14 turns out to be rather simple. It starts with a verification of the exception type, and, if it is of type `NotAuthorized`, the request is forwarded to the login page and that's it (these four lines of code are part of the security system described in the "Security" section of this chapter). If not, the exception is logged and a soothing message is shown to the user.

There are three special cases, though. The first two deal with the fact that `JspException` and `SoftException` contain some stuffing inside and, thus, an extra method call is needed to extract it for proper logging. The third case handles the database exceptions. Because it was decided not to soften `SQLException` at the source (that is, inside `db.StoriesDb` class), it will propagate to this level from all the JSP code that makes database calls directly, namely, from `select.jsp` (see Listing 4.6) and `submit.jsp` (see Listing 4.7). The `Exceptions` aspect has no affect on the JSPs because their generated code is off limits for the AspectJ compiler.

Summary

In this chapter, aspects enabled us to simplify the overall code structure by incorporating the security concern in a code layer separated from business logic. On top of it all, the business code has no explicit connection to the security aspect and does not even suspect that it exists!

The aspects to enforce contracts and to improve the exception handling made our small application much more robust and a little bit simpler. The next step would be to try to improve on development methods.

6

Development Aids

IN THIS CHAPTER

- Logging
- Tracing
- Profiling

The capability of aspects to affect a lot of code at once can help to devise a set of tools to help the application development. This chapter is devoted to building such tools for the AspectNews application.

Logging

The example application was given a built-in logging facility that uses the servlet API exposed by the Init servlet (see Listing 4.10). It gives you the ability to insert a log call any place in the code in a manner similar to System.out.println() calls with output piped to the servlet log file. And, therefore, it is not much of a modular improvement—it is just a logging facility. Aspects make things much more interesting. Consider the following idea:

```
public aspect RigidLogger
{
    pointcut logPoint() : execution(* tags.*.*(..));

    before() : logPoint()
    {
        Init.log(thisJoinPoint),
    }
}
```

This aspect's pointcut logPoint() picks execution (that is, methods' bodies) of all the methods in the tags package, and the before() advice logs their execution as soon as the program's flow reaches them. Note that there is no manual labor involved; it all happens automatically.

This logger idea is nice, but has one big drawback: Whatever is coded in the pointcut `logPoint()` is what will be logged and this is more rigid than desired (hence the name). AspectJ provides a facility to abstract a common functionality that is similar to object-oriented programming, which its aspects can extend classes and other aspects as well as implement interfaces. Aspect extension is limited only to abstract aspects, but this is sufficient to achieve the desired flexibility as far as logging is concerned. Here's an abstract `Logger.java` aspect:

```
package aspects;

import servlets.*;

abstract public aspect Logger
{
    abstract pointcut logPoint();

    before() : logPoint() && !within(Logger+) && !within(Init)
    {
        Init.log(thisJoinPoint.getTarget()+"/"+
                thisJoinPoint.getThis()+"/"+
                thisJoinPoint.getSignature());
    }
}
```

The `Logger` aspect has one vague feature: Its main workhorse pointcut is not specified—it is declared abstract. But the aspect has a very concrete `before()` advice: It logs most of the context available to it including the signature of the join point. But what about custom messages? The AspectJ compiler cannot guess what you have in mind in any particular place (show me the compiler that can!). Therefore, the choices are either to allow the logger to write out what it can gather from the context (such as, signature, target object, this object, and so on—more introspection methods are described in Appendix A, "AspectJ API"), or insert custom log messages manually in precise locations in code.

Note the additional logical pointcut expressions at the advice declaration. It is explicitly set not to fire if the execution flow is inside the logger itself (or its derivatives) or inside the `Init` servlet. The first condition prevents unlimited recursion when the logger advises itself. The second leaves the `Init` servlet off limits because while it is executing on a startup, its `log()` methods are unavailable and will be throwing exceptions because of a lack of servlet context.

Because the `Logger` aspect is abstract, it will not do us any good by itself. It has to be extended with a concrete one. Here are two examples.

Here is the concrete `Logger1.java` aspect:

```
package aspects;

import tags.*;

public aspect Logger1 extends Logger
{
    pointcut logPoint() : execution(* tags.*.*(..));
}
```

And here is the concrete `Logger2.java` aspect:

```
package aspects;

import tags.*;

public aspect Logger2 extends Logger
{
    pointcut logPoint() : staticinitialization(db.*);
}
```

These two concrete aspects actually define previously abstract `logPoint()` pointcut. The first one picks the execution of all methods in package `tags`, the second watches static initialization of classes in package `db`. Executing the AspectNews application with these aspects produces entries in the servlet log file similar to these (they are broken up here to fit the page):

```
2002-01-23 00:22:55 tags.StoriesTag@5e55ab/tags.StoriesTag@5e55ab/int
➥tags.StoriesTag.doStartTag()
2002-01-23 00:22:55 null/null/db.Story.<init>
2002-01-23 00:22:55 tags.StoriesTag@5e55ab/tags.StoriesTag@5e55ab/int
➥tags.StoriesTag.doAfterBody()
2002-01-23 00:22:55 tags.StoriesTag@5e55ab/tags.StoriesTag@5e55ab/int
➥tags.StoriesTag.doAfterBody()
2002-01-23 00:22:55 tags.StoriesTag@5e55ab/tags.StoriesTag@5e55ab/int
➥tags.StoriesTag.doAfterBody()
2002-01-23 00:22:55 tags.StoriesTag@5e55ab/tags.StoriesTag@5e55ab/int
➥tags.StoriesTag.doAfterBody()
2002-01-23 00:22:55 tags.StoriesTag@5e55ab/tags.StoriesTag@5e55ab/int
➥tags.StoriesTag.doAfterBody()
```

What if you finally become annoyed with this voluminous log output and notice that excessive logging does have a hefty performance price tag attached? Because these aspects clearly can be categorized as development aid, they can be turned off or, more precisely, they could never be compiled in. Precise mechanics of doing so is a matter of the development environment. For AspectNews, which is built with Ant, it is sufficient to add a list of files to be excluded to the `exclude` name in the `build.properties` file, for example:

```
exclude=aspects/Logger1.java,aspects/Logger2.java
```

For development builds, the `exclude` name can be commented out thus enabling logging. Turning individual logging aspects on and off at compile time has one advantage over runtime configuration usually utilized with traditional loggers, such as, Apache's log4j package (see `http://jakarta.apache.org/log4j` for details). Although ultimately convenient, these loggers must have executable code in the application, which will execute even if logging is turned off. Despite the fact that this code is relatively small, it all adds up in a complex application resulting in a performance hit. In the case of aspect-based loggers, their code is just not there when they are not compiled in.

You can develop an unlimited number of aspects that extend the abstract Logger. Combining sophisticated pointcuts (see Chapter 11, "Picking Join Points: Pointcuts") with context obtained by reflection API (Appendix A) enables you to have logging at any combination of join points imaginable with varying amount of context printed out and all without ever touching the main application's code. It truly isolates all logging concerns from the rest of the system.

Of course, human beings are still better than computers in making decisions on when and what to log, and the hand-inserted logging code can pinpoint the problem at hand more precisely. But besides a runtime performance penalty mentioned above, manually written log code involves human labor—always an expensive proposition. Aspect-based logger is the equivalent of a mass-produced Chevy versus a hand-crafted Rolls: You lose some refinement, but you can actually afford the result!

Tracing

A good tracer is a very valuable debugging tool, especially in the JSP environment. Although similar to a logger in intent—to see what the application is doing—a tracer has some distinct functional requirements. First of all, a tracer tracks only one type of event—a method execution. Second, it is important to see this execution in the context of a call stack. Third, the tracer's output has to be comprehensible by humans, and it is almost guaranteed to be excessive. The aspect in Listing 6.1 is an attempt to address these requirements.

LISTING 6.1   Tracer.java Aspect

```
package aspects;

import java.util.*;
import servlets.*;

public aspect Tracer
{
    pointcut tracePoint(): execution(* *.*(..))
                           && !within(Tracer) && !within(Init);

    private static Map stackDepths = new HashMap();

    before() : tracePoint()
    {
        Integer depth =
                (Integer)stackDepths.get(Thread.currentThread());
        if( null == depth )
        {
            depth = new Integer(0);
        }
        Init.log(ident(depth.intValue()) + " >> "  +
                    thisJoinPointStaticPart.getSignature());
        stackDepths.put(Thread.currentThread(),
                            new Integer(depth.intValue()+1));
    }

    after() : tracePoint()
    {
        Integer depth =
                (Integer)stackDepths.get(Thread.currentThread());
        depth = new Integer(depth.intValue()-1);
        if( 0 == depth.intValue() )
        {
            stackDepths.remove(Thread.currentThread());
        }
        else
        {
            stackDepths.put(Thread.currentThread(), depth);
        }
        Init.log(ident(depth.intValue()) + " << " +
```

LISTING 6.1   Continued

```
                            thisJoinPointStaticPart.getSignature());
    }

    private static StringBuffer ident(int num)
    {
        StringBuffer ident = new StringBuffer();
        for(int i=0; i<num; i++)
        {
            ident.append(' ');
        }
        ident.append(Integer.toString(num)+
                        " ["+Thread.currentThread().hashCode()+"]");

        return ident;
    }
}
```

The first requirement (the tracing of the method execution) is addressed by the pointcut tracePoint(), which is intended to pick all methods' executions for all classes with all the signatures ever made. As in the case with the Logger.java aspect, the join points within the Init servlet and the Tracer itself are excluded for the same reasons.

The second requirement (*call stack* context) is addressed by a stack depth counter. A simple solution—a static integer variable—will not do you any good because JSP pages are guaranteed (unless configured otherwise) to execute in a multithreaded fashion. Instead of a single counter, you have to create a table of counters—one counter per currently executing thread or, more precisely, one counter per each call stack currently being traced by this aspect. All aspects are, by default, singletons, meaning, there is one instance of each aspect created per running process. This behavior can be changed (see Chapter 10 "Aspects"), therefore, the static declaration of the stackDepths map, although not strictly necessary, is a good precaution against future modification of a singleton policy for this particular aspect. The key for this counter table is the thread object itself—there could not be more than one call stack per thread.

The actual tracing happens in the before() and after() advices of the aspect. In a typical sequence of events the before() advice starts executing first, as soon as a method is picked by the tracePoint() pointcut. The two possibilities are first, that there is an existing call stack and, in this case, its counter is sitting in the stackDepth table. Second, the execution flow is at the top level, meaning this is the first layer of code advised by the `Tracer` aspect and the depth counter has to be created. Because the counter is to be stored in the map, it cannot be an intrinsic type, but rather an object wrapper `Integer`.

Next, the `Init.log()` method is used to write out the tracing information to the log file. It uses three pieces of tracing information: the stack depth value, the direction of the execution flow (inward `">>"`), and the signature of the method at the join point. A utility method, `ident(int)`, was developed to address the third requirement for a good tracer— comprehensibility. It formats a log string that contains a properly indented stack depth and a thread's hash code, so traces from different threads can be distinguished. The `before()` advice concludes by incrementing the depth counter and saving it to the depth counters table.

The `after()` advice unwinds in a reverse fashion. First, the depth counter is obtained from the table and it has to be there or else. Second, its value is decremented. If it reaches zero, it means that you are at the top of the stack and this is the end of this particular trace, and the counter has to be removed from the table. Because you do not have any control over thread allocation policy of the servlet container (short of configuring some minimal and maximum numbers of threads in thread pools), this also serves as a garbage collection mechanism for the counter table. If nothing is currently being traced, there is no counter for it regardless of the thread's existence. The advice finishes by writing the log string as described previously. Here is the example of the log output (lines are broken up to fit the page):

```
2002-01-26 15:05:43 0 [7279485] >>
➡PageContext security.TagSupport.getPageContext()
2002-01-26 15:05:43 0 [7279485] <<
➡PageContext security.TagSupport.getPageContext()
2002-01-26 15:05:54 0 [6729651] >>
➡void servlets.Register.doPost(HttpServletRequest, HttpServletResponse)
2002-01-26 15:05:54 0 [6729651] <<
➡void servlets.Register.doPost(HttpServletRequest, HttpServletResponse)
2002-01-26 15:05:54 0 [7279485] >>
➡PageContext security.TagSupport.getPageContext()
2002-01-26 15:05:54 0 [7279485] <<
➡PageContext security.TagSupport.getPageContext()
2002-01-26 15:05:54 0 [7279485] >>
➡int tags.UserTag.doStartTag()
2002-01-26 15:05:54 0 [7279485] <<
➡int tags.UserTag.doStartTag()
2002-01-26 15:05:54 0 [7279485] >>
➡int tags.UserTag.doEndTag()
2002-01-26 15:05:54 0 [7279485] <<
➡int tags.UserTag.doEndTag()
```

```
2002-01-26 15:05:56 0 [6729651] >>
➥void tags.StoriesTag.setName(String)
2002-01-26 15:05:56 0 [6729651] <<
➥void tags.StoriesTag.setName(String)
2002-01-26 15:05:56 0 [6729651] >>
➥PageContext security.BodyTagSupport.getPageContext()
2002-01-26 15:05:56 0 [6729651] <<
➥PageContext security.BodyTagSupport.getPageContext()
2002-01-26 15:05:56 0 [6729651] >>
 ➥int tags.StoriesTag.doStartTag()
2002-01-26 15:05:56  1 [6729651] >>
➥Collection db.StoriesDb.retrieve(String)
2002-01-26 15:05:56  1 [6729651] <<
➥Collection db.StoriesDb.retrieve(String)
2002-01-26 15:05:56 0 [6729651] <<
➥int tags.StoriesTag.doStartTag()
2002-01-26 15:05:56 0 [6729651] >>
➥int tags.StoriesTag.doAfterBody()
2002-01-26 15:05:56 0 [6729651] <<
 ➥int tags.StoriesTag.doAfterBody()
```

As you can see, two threads are responsible for executing the client's request; their hash codes are 7279485 and 6729651, respectively. If these codes were not there, it would be difficult to make sense of the execution flow. Because the AspectNews application is really simple, the deepest point of the call stack is 2, which is reached when db.StoriesDb.retrieve(String) is called from tags.StoriesTag.doStartTag(). The indentation of the output is best appreciated when the call stack grows more than 5 levels deep.

The same compilation strategy described for the Logger aspect can be applied to the Tracer—it should not be compiled in if not needed.

Profiling

Because you already have a usable tracer, it is a trivial exercise to convert it to a profiler—a tool that will time the execution of application's methods. One major change is to replace the stack depths table with a call tree and keep execution statistics in the tree's branches. Real profilers prefer to store profiling information separately from the profiled process in order to separate data collection from analysis. Let's go with the flow and write profiling information to a file.

Let's look at the tracer output first. Theoretically, you can construct a program that will be capable of analyzing the tracer output and derive the timing information. Unfortunately, tracer's output has some disadvantages as a profiler's data store:

- The time stamping is not granular enough. The servlet logger stamps its output down to a second and that is not nearly sufficient.

- The tracer logs only execution of the advised methods, the profiler would need method calls.

- Pretty formatting, although convenient for humans, is a nuisance for a profiler tool.

All these considerations lead to the `Profiler` aspect shown in Listing 6.2). It writes out time stamps before and after each method call in all the advised code.

LISTING 6.2   `Profiler.java` Aspect

```
package aspects;

import java.io.*;
import org.aspectj.lang.SoftException;

public aspect Profiler
{
    pointcut prof(): call(* *.*(..)) && !within(aspects.*);

    FileOutputStream out;

    public Profiler() throws FileNotFoundException
    {
        out = new FileOutputStream("profile.txt");
    }

    before() : prof()
    {
        String record = "+ " +
            Thread.currentThread().hashCode()+" "+
            Long.toString(System.currentTimeMillis())+" "+
            thisJoinPointStaticPart.getSignature()+"\n";

        try
        {
            out.write(record.getBytes());
        }
```

LISTING 6.2   Continued

```
        catch(IOException e)
        {
            throw new SoftException(e);
        }
    }

    after() : prof()
    {
        String record ="- "+
          Thread.currentThread().hashCode()+" "+
          Long.toString(System.currentTimeMillis())+" "+
          thisJoinPointStaticPart.getSignature()+"\n";

        try
        {
            out.write(record.getBytes());
        }
        catch(IOException e)
        {
            throw new SoftException(e);
        }
    }
}
```

The main pointcut of this aspect also excludes this and all other aspects from profiling. Of course, anything can be included by modifying the prof() pointcut definition, but be aware of unlimited recursions.

The collected timestamps will be written to a file stream defined as an aspect variable and opened in the aspect's constructor. An aspect can have one (and only one) constructor that does not take any arguments; this is a good place to put some relevant initialization code. The reasons why the raw output stream was chosen over more convenient, and possibly buffered print writer, will become apparent in Chapter 7, "Runtime Improvements," but believe me for now, it has to do more with exhibitionism than masochism. The output filename can be configured in and obtained from the Web application descriptor, but for simplicity's sake, it is just hard coded here (Java creates it in its current directory by default).

Both before() and after() advices both time stamp their respective join points, and their output differs only by one character: + in before() and - in after(). Because Profiler's advices perform raw output operations, their exceptions have to be handled somehow. Generally, an advice can declare and throw an exception. The caveat is that all exceptions thrown by advices must correspond to the exceptions expected at each target join point.

As was shown in Part I of this book, the advices are translated to method calls inside some target code. If this target code does not include any handling for a particular exception, the compilation error will result. This is exactly the case with `FileOutputStream.write()` method—it throws an `IOException` that either has to be consumed inside of the advice or thrown further. Consuming exceptions in place goes against the spirit of aspect-oriented programming, so the exception has to be rethrown. It will be rethrown as AspectJ's `org.aspectj.lang.SoftException`, which is specially designed for this purpose. This exception extends `java.lang.RuntimeException` and, as such, it does not have to be declared. If `IOException` is thrown refer to Chapter 5, "Crosscutting by Design," where the modular strategy of exception handling with AspectJ was discussed.

The fragment of the `profile.txt` file that contains the aspect's output is presented here:

```
+ 2149462 1012150720471
⮕String servlets.Init.getParameter(String)
+ 2149462 1012150720471
⮕String javax.servlet.ServletContext.getInitParameter(String)
2149462 1012150720471
⮕String javax.servlet.ServletContext.getInitParameter(String)
- 2149462 1012150720471
⮕String servlets.Init.getParameter(String)
+ 2149462 1012150720471
⮕Class java.lang.Class.forName(String)
- 2149462 1012150720481
⮕Class java.lang.Class.forName(String)
+ 2149462 1012150720481
⮕Object java.lang.Class.newInstance()
- 2149462 1012150720481
⮕Object java.lang.Class.newInstance()
+ 4254871 1012150740630
⮕void javax.servlet.ServletContext.log(String)
- 4254871 1012150740630
 ⮕void javax.servlet.ServletContext.log(String)
+ 4254871 1012150740640
⮕void javax.servlet.ServletContext.log(String)
- 4254871 1012150740640
⮕void javax.servlet.ServletContext.log(String)
```

```
+ 4254871 1012150740640
➥void javax.servlet.ServletContext.log(String)
- 4254871 1012150740640
➥void javax.servlet.ServletContext.log(String)
+ 4254871 1012150740660
➥Object org.aspectj.lang.JoinPoint.getTarget()
- 4254871 1012150740660
➥Object org.aspectj.lang.JoinPoint.getTarget()
+ 4254871 1012150740670
➥PageContext security.BodyTagSupport.getPageContext()
+ 4254871 1012150740670
➥void javax.servlet.ServletContext.log(String)
- 4254871 1012150740670
➥void javax.servlet.ServletContext.log(String)
+ 4254871 1012150740670
➥void javax.servlet.ServletContext.log(String)
- 4254871 1012150740670
➥void javax.servlet.ServletContext.log(String)
- 4254871 1012150740670
 ➥PageContext security.BodyTagSupport.getPageContext()
```

A simple Perl implementation of an actual profiler tool is presented in Listing 6.3.

LISTING 6.3   `profiler.pl` Profiler Script

```perl
while(<>)
{
    next if /^\*\*\*\*/;
    chop;
    ($direction, $thread, $stamp, $method) = split(/ /, $_, 4);

    @stack = @{$threads{$thread}};
    if( $direction eq "+" )
    {
        push @stack, $stamp;
        $threads{$thread} = [@stack];
    }
    else
    {
        $elapsed = $stamp - pop @stack;
        $methods{$method} =
          [($methods{$method}[0]+1, $methods{$method}[1]+$elapsed)];
```

LISTING 6.3   Continued

```
    }
}

foreach $method (sort keys %methods)
{
    $totalTime += $methods{$method}[1];

    printf "%6d %6.2f %s\n",
      $methods{$method}[0],
      $methods{$method}[1]/$methods{$method}[0],
      $method;
}
print "Total: $totalTime\n";
```

It contains two loops: The while() loop iterates over the output file (presumed to be piped in), parses profile records, and builds %methods hash. Each element of this hash is itself an array containing a counter of invocations and the total time spent in a method. The key to the hash is the method name. The second loop just prints out the content of the %methods hash when all profile records are read.

Its output looks like this:

```
 31    9.06 ResultSet java.sql.Statement.executeQuery(String)
104    0.00 String javax.servlet.ServletContext.getInitParameter(String)
  1  110.00 Connection java.sql.DriverManager.getConnection(String, String, String)
321    0.12 void javax.servlet.jsp.PageContext.setAttribute(String, Object)
  1    0.00 Enumeration javax.servlet.ServletContext.getInitParameterNames()
  8    0.00 void javax.servlet.jsp.JspWriter.print(String)
321    0.16 JspWriter javax.servlet.jsp.tagext.BodyTagSupport.getPreviousOut()
  1   10.00 void javax.servlet.http.HttpSession.setAttribute(String, Object)
656    0.21 String java.sql.ResultSet.getString(int)
429    0.58 void javax.servlet.ServletContext.log(String)
365    0.11 boolean java.sql.ResultSet.next()
334    0.06 boolean java.util.Collection.add(Object)
  1   10.00 Class java.lang.Class.forName(String)
 33    0.00 Statement java.sql.Connection.createStatement()
 73    0.00 Object javax.servlet.http.HttpSession.getAttribute(String)
  2    0.00 ServletRequest javax.servlet.jsp.PageContext.getRequest()
 27    0.74 Iterator java.util.Collection.iterator()
  9    0.00 PageContext security.TagSupport.getPageContext()
  5    0.00 int java.sql.Statement.executeUpdate(String)
```

```
321    0.16 void javax.servlet.jsp.tagext.BodyContent.clearBody()
  1    0.00 boolean java.lang.String.equals(Object)
  1   60.00 ServletContext javax.servlet.GenericServlet.getServletContext()
324    0.19 Object java.util.Iterator.next()
321    0.19 void javax.servlet.jsp.tagext.BodyContent.writeOut(Writer)
104    0.19 String servlets.Init.getParameter(String)
  1    0.00 boolean security.UsersDb.check(String, String)
 26    0.00 Collection db.StoriesDb.retrieve(String)
  1    0.00 Object java.lang.Class.newInstance()
  4    2.50 String javax.servlet.ServletRequest.getParameter(String)
 26    0.38 PageContext security.BodyTagSupport.getPageContext()
 35    0.29 Object org.aspectj.lang.JoinPoint.getTarget()
 70    0.00 HttpSession javax.servlet.jsp.PageContext.getSession()
351    0.11 boolean java.util.Iterator.hasNext()
  4    0.00 Object java.util.Enumeration.nextElement()
321    0.03 BodyContent javax.servlet.jsp.tagext.BodyTagSupport.getBodyContent()
  5    0.00 boolean java.util.Enumeration.hasMoreElements()
  4    2.50 void servlets.Init.log(String)
  8    0.00 JspWriter javax.servlet.jsp.PageContext.getOut()
```

The left-most column contains the number of times any given method was invoked, the second column shows an average time the program has spent executing it, and the last column is the method name. Please note that this report corresponds only to the portion of the profile.txt file that was actually fed to the profiler script. This is why not all the methods of the AspectNews application are represented and some undoubtedly popular methods (such as, java.lang.String.equals(Object)) show only a single invocation.

Summary

These aspects cleanly and transparently allow us to get a better handle on what is going on with the application. Because we can now measure runtime characteristics of the application, it would be possible to try to improve them and measure the result.

Runtime Improvements

This chapter explores various ways to improve runtime characteristics of the AspectNews application. Given the crosscutting nature of most of them, the aspects can be an effective and domain-independent solution.

Buffering

One of the reasons the Profiler aspect (see Listing 6.2) did not use a buffered print writer is that buffering is too good of an example of aspects' use to pass on. Of course, there are more useful and less contrived examples of buffering than file streams—they are already implemented (albeit, differently) inside the Java standard library, but our examples have to stay relatively compact to be useful in a book.

In the AspectNews application the Profiler aspect is the only place where output stream is used. However, the discussion in this chapter applies equally to the situation where file streams are scattered throughout code and are an integral part of the application's design. The first and wrong idea of addressing buffering concern might look like Listing 7.1.

LISTING 7.1   First Attempt to Implement a Buffering Aspect

```
package wrong;

import java.io.*;

public aspect WrongBuffering1
{
    private static final int BUFF_SIZE=256;
```

LISTING 7.1   Continued

```
    byte[] buff = new byte[BUFF_SIZE];
    int counter = 0;

    pointcut writeBytes(byte[] bytes):
    call(void FileOutputStream.write(byte[]))
    && args(bytes)
    && !within(WrongBuffering1);

    void around(byte[] bytes) throws IOException: writeBytes(bytes)
    {
        FileOutputStream out =
          (FileOutputStream)thisJoinPoint.getTarget();
        if(counter + bytes.length > BUFF_SIZE)
        {
            out.write(buff, 0, counter);
            out.write(bytes);

            counter=0;
        }
        else
        {
            System.arraycopy(bytes, 0, buff, counter, bytes.length);
            counter += bytes.length;
        }
    }
}
```

The pointcut `writeBytes()` picks all calls to `FileOutputStream.write(byte[])` method, and the `around()` advice runs instead of them. The pointcut declares one argument—an array of bytes to be written, which gets passed to the advice for buffering. The `within()` pointcut prevents an unlimited recursion. The advice receives a byte array and decides what to do with it. If the internal buffer is almost full, it is written out along with the byte array just received. If not, the byte array is copied to the end of the buffer and no physical writing occurs.

There is an obvious problem, though. The underlying `FileOutputStream` is obtained as the join point's target, which is correct. What is not correct is that there will be as many targets as instances of `FileOutputStream` class throughout the program and only one instance of the aspect. By default, AspectJ creates one instance of an aspect per Java runtime. In this particular case, it causes the content of all these streams to be mixed in the buffer and to be written into essentially random files (whatever stream happens to be the target at the time the buffer fills up). AspectJ allows you to change the default aspect instantiation policy, now, in addition to singleton aspects (the default), aspects can be created on per this, per target, or per control flow basis. While deferring the general aspect allocation discussion until Chapter 10, it is worth pointing that for buffering solution the perthis aspect is best suited, meaning, a buffering aspect will be allocated for each instance of the target—a FileOutputStream. The idea leads to the second attempt at a buffering implementation in Listing 7.2.

LISTING 7.2   Second Attempt to Implement a Buffering Aspect

```
package wrong;

import java.io.*;

public aspect WrongBuffering2 pertarget(target(FileOutputStream))
{
    private static final int BUFF_SIZE=256;
    byte[] buff = new byte[BUFF_SIZE];
    int counter = 0;

    pointcut writeBytes(byte[] bytes):
    call(void FileOutputStream.write(byte[]))
    && args(bytes)
    && !within(WrongBuffering2);

    void around(byte[] bytes) throws IOException: writeBytes(bytes)
    {
        FileOutputStream out =
          (FileOutputStream)thisJoinPoint.getTarget();
        WrongBuffering2 wb = WrongBuffering2.aspectOf(out);
        if(wb.counter + bytes.length > BUFF_SIZE)
        {
            out.write(wb.buff, 0, wb.counter);
            out.write(bytes);

            wb.counter=0;
        }
        else
        {
            System.arraycopy(bytes, 0, wb.buff,
                                    wb.counter, bytes.length);
```

LISTING 7.2   Continued

```
            wb.counter += bytes.length;
        }
    }
}
```

This time around everything seems to be just perfect. The output stream can still be accessed as the join point's target, but because now each target has its own aspect, the latter has to be obtained separately. The API for it is provided in the form of `anAspect.aspectOf(Object)` and this method call yields an aspect's instance associated with the object in question. The instance variables for the aspect's instance can be addressed in a usual Java manner—now each `FileOutputStream` has its own aspect and, therefore, its own buffer and counter. If only it worked.

The reason it does not is rather fundamental: To create a `pertarget` aspect, AspectJ has to have access to the source code of the target, which, for most practical purposes, in this case is unavailable. Theoretically speaking, the compiled Java byte codes can be used for interweaving aspects into them in pretty much the same manner the source code can. Whether or not it is a good idea to advise a third-party library for which no source is available is, at the time of this writing, the subject of an animated debate that borders on a flame war.

However, because the basic idea behind a buffering aspect is now apparent, the per target (that is, per stream) buffering can be implemented "manually" or, in other words, using one singleton aspect and a table of buffers inside of it (see Listing 7.3).

LISTING 7.3   `OutputStreamBuffering.java` Aspect

```
package aspects;

import java.io.*;
import java.util.*;

public aspect OutputStreamBuffering implements Runnable
{
    private static Thread flushingThread = null;

    private static final int BUFF_SIZE=512;
    public class Buffer
    {
        byte[] buff = null;
        int counter = 0;
```

LISTING 7.3   Continued

```
    Buffer()
    {
        buff = new byte[BUFF_SIZE];
    }
}

private Map buffTable = new HashMap();

pointcut writeBytes(byte[] bytes):
call(void FileOutputStream.write(byte[]))
&& args(bytes)
&& !within(OutputStreamBuffering);

void around(byte[] bytes) throws IOException: writeBytes(bytes)
{
    FileOutputStream out =
                    (FileOutputStream)thisJoinPoint.getTarget();
    Buffer aBuff = (Buffer) buffTable.get(out);
    if( null == aBuff )
    {
        aBuff = new Buffer();
        buffTable.put(out, aBuff);
    }

    if(aBuff.counter + bytes.length > BUFF_SIZE)
    {
        synchronized(out)
        {
            out.write(aBuff.buff, 0, aBuff.counter);
            out.write(bytes);
            out.write(("*** buffer - "+aBuff.counter +
                                            "\n").getBytes());
        }

        buffTable.remove(out);
    }
    else
    {
        System.arraycopy(bytes, 0, aBuff.buff,
                                aBuff.counter, bytes.length);
```

LISTING 7.3   Continued

```
                aBuff.counter += bytes.length;
        }

        if( null == flushingThread )
        {
            flushingThread = new Thread(this);
            flushingThread.setDaemon(true);
            flushingThread.start();
        }

    }

    before() throws IOException : call(void FileOutputStream.close())
    {
        FileOutputStream out =
                        (FileOutputStream)thisJoinPoint.getTarget();
        Buffer aBuff = (Buffer) buffTable.get(out);
        if( null != aBuff )
        {
            synchronized(out)
            {
                out.write(aBuff.buff, 0, aBuff.counter);
            }
            buffTable.remove(out);
        }
    }

    public void run()
    {
        while(true)
        {
            try
            {
                Thread.sleep(3000);
                flush();
            }
            catch(Throwable e)
            {
            }
        }
    }
```

LISTING 7.3 Continued

```
void flush() throws IOException
{
    for(Iterator i=buffTable.keySet().iterator(); i.hasNext(); )
    {
        FileOutputStream out = (FileOutputStream)i.next();
        Buffer aBuff = (Buffer) buffTable.get(out);
        synchronized(out)
        {
            out.write(aBuff.buff, 0, aBuff.counter);
            out.write(("*** flushed - "+aBuff.counter +
                                        "\n").getBytes());
        }
        i.remove();
    }
}

protected void finalize() throws Throwable
{
    flush();
    super.finalize();
}
}
```

As is usually the case, the real implementation got a little bit more complicated than the original idea implied. The first complication is that besides the internal buffer itself, a size counter is needed. A variable size structure such as java.util.Vector can be used, but it would be far less efficient. The fixed size buffer utilized in the previous aspect does not have to be resized, and copying into it is a low-level operation that is implemented (hopefully) by the Java runtime system on the operating system level. An inner class Buffer is declared to bundle the buffer and its counter together. Instances of this class are stored in the buffers' table buffTable, one for each FileOutputStream object.

The second complication arises from the fact that there is no explicit flushing as in the case of regular Java buffered streams. In the latter case, the flushing of the stream is the concern of an application programmer: The buffer has to be either explicitly flushed or it will be flushed automatically upon file closing. Because the aspect takes care of buffering concerns, the automatic "behind the scene" flushing has to be provided. This concern is implemented in three parts:

1. The aspect itself is declared to implement the Runnable interface and it starts itself as a separate thread at the first opportunity to do so—after the first attempt to buffer the output. The run() method loops continuously and periodically calls the internal flush() method. This method scans the table of buffers and writes them out.

2. The finalize() method flushes the buffers.

3. If the stream will be explicitly closed, a before() advice flushes it before closing proceeds.

There are also a couple of debugging output statements to indicate in the output file that buffering is actually happening. Compare the following to the original (not buffered) version of the profile.txt file shown in Chapter 6:

```
- 2149462 1012581837072 void servlets.Init.log(String)
+ 2149462 1012581837072 boolean java.util.Enumeration.hasMoreElements()
- 2149462 1012581837072 boolean java.util.Enumeration.hasMoreElements()
+ 2149462 1012581837072 Object java.util.Enumeration.nextElement()
- 2149462 1012581837072 Object java.util.Enumeration.nextElement()
+ 2149462 1012581837072 String servlets.Init.getParameter(String)
+ 2149462 1012581837072
        String javax.servlet.ServletContext.getInitParameter(String)
- 2149462 1012581837072
        String javax.servlet.ServletContext.getInitParameter(String)
*** buffer - 484
- 2149462 1012581837072 String servlets.Init.getParameter(String)
+ 2149462 1012581837072 void servlets.Init.log(String)
+ 2149462 1012581837072 void javax.servlet.ServletContext.log(String)
- 2149462 1012581837072 void javax.servlet.ServletContext.log(String)
- 2149462 1012581837072 void servlets.Init.log(String)
+ 2149462 1012581837072 boolean java.util.Enumeration.hasMoreElements()
- 2149462 1012581837072 boolean java.util.Enumeration.hasMoreElements()
+ 2149462 1012581837072 String servlets.Init.getParameter(String)
*** buffer - 460
+ 2149462 1012581837072
        String javax.servlet.ServletContext.getInitParameter(String)
- 2149462 1012581837072
        String javax.servlet.ServletContext.getInitParameter(String)
- 2149462 1012581837072 String servlets.Init.getParameter(String)
+ 2149462 1012581837072 Class java.lang.Class.forName(String)
- 2149462 1012581837082 Class java.lang.Class.forName(String)
+ 2149462 1012581837082 Object java.lang.Class.newInstance()
- 2149462 1012581837082 Object java.lang.Class.newInstance()
*** flushed - 482
```

The third complication is that the aspect can (and should) use synchronization that is a little bit more diligent—it was omitted for clarity's sake.

There are also a couple of practical considerations. First, to be useful, the aspect needs an adjustment of the buffer size and the frequency of flushing for optimal performance. The values set in the previous example (512 bytes and every 3 seconds, respectively) are probably too small. Second, the possible recursive calling conditions have to be monitored. Consider what happens if the tracing is turned on (see the section "Tracing" in Chapter 6). The Tracer aspect will advise the flush() method of the OutputStreamBuffering aspect and insert some code to call a logging method to record the trace. This fact will be picked by the Profiler that will, in turn, try to write the execution statistics into its output stream. That will fill the stream buffer in the OutputStreamBuffering aspect and it has to be flushed again despite the fact that nothing meaningful is happening. The program will keep writing the profile information forever:

```
+ 6056567 1012578319734 void javax.servlet.ServletContext.log(String)
- 6056567 1012578319734 void javax.servlet.ServletContext.log(String)
+ 6056567 1012578322739 void javax.servlet.ServletContext.log(String)
- 6056567 1012578322739 void javax.servlet.ServletContext.log(String)
*** flushed - 280
+ 6056567 1012578322739 void javax.servlet.ServletContext.log(String)
- 6056567 1012578322739 void javax.servlet.ServletContext.log(String)
+ 6056567 1012578325743 void javax.servlet.ServletContext.log(String)
- 6056567 1012578325743 void javax.servlet.ServletContext.log(String)
*** flushed - 280
+ 6056567 1012578325743 void javax.servlet.ServletContext.log(String)
- 6056567 1012578325743 void javax.servlet.ServletContext.log(String)
+ 6056567 1012578328747 void javax.servlet.ServletContext.log(String)
- 6056567 1012578328747 void javax.servlet.ServletContext.log(String)
*** flushed - 280
```

The solution is either to modify the Tracer aspect to leave the OutputStreamBuffering alone or not to include both of them into the same production system. The development runs should be just fine as long as they aren't left unattended for any extended period of time, continuous logging will ultimately fill up the file system (no, it did not happen to me).

Pooling

One of the biggest time savers in database-related code is the capability to pool the database connections, which is, probably, the most time consuming operation. In the AspectNews application, each database method gets a JDBC connection from the driver manager at the beginning (see, for example, Listing 4.11, Listing 5.7, or Listing 5.9). Pooling of the database connections means that several connections will always be open at the same time, and they will be dispensed as needed from some shared pool. The idea is so appealing that it has made its way into official JDBC specification v.3 (`http://java.sun.com/products/jdbc/download.html`). But there is no need to wait until the database vendor of your choice catches up with the spec. Because the pooling exhibits all the properties of a crosscutting concern, it should be easy to implement with an aspect (see Listing 7.4).

LISTING 7.4   Pooling.java Aspect

```
package aspects;

import java.sql.*;
import java.util.*;

public aspect Pooling
{
    private static Stack pool = new Stack();

    pointcut poolGet():
        call(static Connection DriverManager.getConnection(..));
    pointcut poolPut():
        call(void Connection.close());

    Connection around() throws SQLException: poolGet()
    {
        synchronized(pool)
        {
            if(pool.empty())
            {
                return proceed();
            }
            return (Connection)pool.pop();
        }
    }

    void around(): poolPut()
    {
        Connection conn = (Connection)thisJoinPoint.getTarget();
        pool.push(conn);
    }
}
```

In this aspect the pooled JDBC connections are kept in the bottomless stack pool. The pointcut `poolGet()` picks all calls that can create database connections, and the pointcut `poolPut()` picks the opposites—the calls that close them. These two point-cuts trigger their respective `around()` advices that perform complementary opera-tions of getting connections in and out of the pool. When an application tries to obtain a connection, the first advice runs. If the pool is empty, as it would be initially, or when all connections are dispensed from it, the new connection is obtained by allowing to `proceed()`. If there is a connection in the pool, the advice pops the pool stack and returns the result. The second advice pushes join point's target—the connection—back to the stack.

There is no limitation on how many connections can be pooled—they are created as long as stack is empty. Eventually, they all will be pushed back into the stack; it just grows in size as needed. Granted, it is not a very prudent strategy, especially if the system gets overloaded with concurrent requests, but it is a reasonable first working version (more details on pooling are available in Ivan Kiselev, "Resource Pooling in Java," *Java Developers Journal*, November 2000: 22-28). Speaking of concurrency, it appears that there is no need for any special measures because the `java.util.Stack` is a subclass of `Vector`, which is synchronized. Unfortunately, the running thread can be preempted between calls to `pool.empty()` and `pool.pop()`, which could be a problem if there will be only one connection left in the pool. Therefore, this section of the first `around()` advice has to have a synchronized access to the pool.

Now, when a pooling concern is addressed (albeit somewhat simplistically), let's consider what happens at the runtime. The hope is that the application eventually will accumulate enough connections in the pool to sustain a normal operational pattern without ever requesting a new database connection from the driver. It would be fantastic if the database connections stayed in perfect shape forever. Unfortunately, they do go bad on a regular basis, specifically, if the database is restarted. Is it a good reason for concern? Absolutely, if connections get spoiled in the pool, the only way to fix them is to restart the whole application. But is it a crosscutting concern? This depends on the context. In the case limited to database connections only, it is not—connections can be checked when dispensed out of the pool and this is the end of it. But let's consider the issue more broadly. The `Pooling` aspect can easily be made abstract in the manner discussed in Chapter 6 in the section "Logging." Then, the concrete aspects can be written for each connection kind: JDBC, CORBA, RMI, or any other kind of limited resource to be pooled, not even necessarily a connection. In this case, these two concerns—resource pooling and the quality of the pooled resource—are separate and should be modularized as distinct concerns.

Keeping in mind that the discussion in this chapter is applicable to any kind of resource (not only to database connections), we can now express the connection quality concern in a separate aspect (see Listing 7.5).

LISTING 7.5   `ConnectionChecking.java` Aspect

```java
package aspects;

import java.sql.*;
import java.util.*;

public aspect ConnectionChecking dominates Pooling
{
    Connection around() throws SQLException:
            call(static Connection DriverManager.getConnection(..))
    {
        Connection conn;
        do
        {
            conn = proceed();
        }
        while(bad(conn));

        return conn;
    }

    private boolean bad(Connection conn)
    {
        try
        {
            Statement stmt = conn.createStatement();
            ResultSet rs = stmt.executeQuery("SELECT 2+2");

            if(rs.next())
            {
                rs.getString(1);
            }
            rs.close();
            stmt.close();
        }
        catch(SQLException e)
        {
            return true;
        }
        return false;
    }
}
```

The aspect executes its around() advice when the application tries to get a database connection (the pointcut is anonymous for a change). The advice just proceeds with whatever was the call to get the connection and calls its private bad() method to check whether the connection is any good. The method just executes a dummy SQL statement (it might not work in this form for your particular database, so try it from your database client tool first). If the statement succeeds, the connection is deemed good, and bad otherwise. On the latter case the advice will keep trying to obtain the connection while the bad ones will be discarded and left at the mercy of the garbage collector. The three possibilities are

- The database is stopped and, thus, unavailable. It means that all connections in the pool are bad and no new ones can be created. The while() loop in the advice then will exhaust all connections from the pool, thus forcing the pool to try to create a new one. The create operation will fail, and the SQLException will propagate through proceed() operations and will eventually be thrown to the caller in the application.

- The database has been restarted and all connections in the pool are bad. The same scenario as above will play out with the exception that the new connection will be created successfully and returned from the driver to the pool and to the ConnectionChecking aspect.

- The database has been restarted and some connections in the pool are bad. The while() loop and bad() method will keep discarding connections until the good one is found. It then will be returned.

As you probably noticed, all this wonderful functionality depends on the fact that the ConnectionChecking aspect executes its advice before Pooling does. Consider what would happen if it was the opposite and Pooling's proceed() preceded ConnectionChecking's one. When the connection is obtained from the pool's stack, there is no proceed() at all and, thus, no connection checking will occur. When the pool is empty, the ConnectionChecking aspect will check a connection freshly obtained from the driver, which is guaranteed to be good. Overall, it is just the opposite of what was really intended.

AspectJ does not provide any default rule with regard to the order of aspect application. Fortunately, there is a way to force what is needed: a dominates keyword in aspect declaration (see Listing 7.6) that tells the AspectJ compiler that the aspect has the precedence. Indeed, the ConnectionChecking aspect has to be applied before anything else (including Pooling): The connections have to be good no matter what their source is, meaning, they all have to be checked before the application gets them. In this example, all connections are checked whether they are coming from the internal pool or were just obtained from the driver.

Caching

After connection pooling, the next step in the never-ending quest for performance improvement is caching—a strategy to avoid hitting the database by all possible means. For the AspectNews application we will implement a read cache of news stories.

But is it a real crosscutting concern or is it just a narrow focused performance improvement trick? Or, to phrase it in a language introduced in the article "Aspect-Oriented Programming" by Kiczales et al (see Appendix F, "References"), can it be "… cleanly encapsulated in a generalized procedure?" The answer is probably, no. The reason is because while all caching algorithms are rather generic, the I/O methods are not. In fact, they do depend on the kind of information being cached. For example, low-level disk cache deals with byte arrays and their physical position on a disk, a database handles data records (also a well-known and distinct structure), and so on. Looking from an implementation point of view, it is rather difficult to devise an aspect that, while crosscutting in nature, will be able to handle all interesting kinds of data. In the case of AspectNews, for example, the operations on stories differ from operations on permissions—a universal facility has to know the difference in method signatures, table layouts, and other intimate details of these data structures.

So, in my humble opinion, the aspect in Listing 7.6 does not exhibit enough cross-cutting properties to address a true concern of this application. But, if we have such a powerful tool as AspectJ, should we be constrained by philosophical considerations? Basically, we want to improve the application performance by transparently implementing caching functionality and separating it from the business logic. And we have a tool to do it. Moreover, it would be a shame if we could not—let's go for it then.

LISTING 7.6   ReadCache.java Aspect

```
package aspects;

import java.sql.*;
import java.util.*;

public aspect ReadCache
{
    private static Map cache = new Hashtable();

    pointcut read(String user):
    call(Collection StoriesDb.retrieve(String)) && args(user);
```

LISTING 7.6   Continued

```
pointcut dirtyUser(String user):
call(* StoriesDb.savePreferences(String, ..)) && args(user);

pointcut dirtyAll():
call(* StoriesDb.saveStory(..));

Collection around(String user) throws SQLException: read(user)
{
    Collection res = (Collection)cache.get(user);
    if(null == res)
    {
        res = proceed();
        cache.put(user, res);
    }
    return res;
}

after(String user): dirtyUser(user)
{
    cache.remove(user);
}

after(): dirtyAll()
{
    cache.clear();
}
}
```

The cache itself is represented as a Map keyed by user IDs. Pointcut read() picks calls to StoriesDb.retrieve(String user); the corresponding around() advice either fetches stories from the cache or retrieves them from the database by proceeding. Freshly retrieved stories are put in cache afterwards. The read() pointcut and the around() advice that it triggers, obviously, need a parameter—user ID—by which the stories are kept in the cache and it is picked by the args() primitive pointcut.

The cached stories are good practically forever or until the information in the database changes—whatever comes first. My bet will be on the database. Two events can invalidate the set of stories currently in the cache: Either the user changes his preferences (by calling StoriesDb.savePreferences()), or somebody submits a new story (by calling StoriesDb.saveStory()). In the first case, the stories in the cache either contain subjects not relevant anymore or miss newly added categories. In the second case, a newly added story might be of interest to the current user, but he will not see it because it was created after the cache was populated. Fortunately, both cases can be picked by simple pointcuts `dirtyUser()` and `dirtyAll()`.

These cases affect the cache differently. First, it affects only one user at a time, when this particular user changes his preferences. The corresponding `after()` advice removes cached stories for this user only. When the story collection changes, it invalidates the cache for all users because there is no way of knowing for what users this story will be relevant (well, at least, no simple way). In this case, the `after()` advice that is triggered by the `dirtyAll()` pointcut just clears the cache completely.

Summary

In this chapter we have seen examples of the aspects' use in implementing popular runtime improvement methods. Although our implementations happened not to be as domain independent as we would like, it is, nevertheless, an improvement over just a callable library. We have managed to change the runtime characteristics of the application without affecting its business logic on the code level.

In the next two chapters we will examine aspects' suitability to accommodate major changes in the application's environment and will try to measure aspects' runtime impact.

8

Coping with Change

IN THIS CHAPTER

• New Logging

• New Levels of Service

As mentioned before, the whole idea behind aspect-oriented programming is modularization. It is supposed to make programs easier to develop and maintain. In this chapter we will consider what will happen if the world around the AspectNews application were to suddenly change, and how what we have done so far with aspects will help us to cope.

New Logging

Let's assume, for the sake of argument, that from now on the AspectNews application will become a part of a big network-management infrastructure. Among other things, it means that our logging mechanism that uses servlets' API (see the "Logging" section in Chapter 6) is no longer sufficient, and a new network-aware logging mechanism is required.

The obvious solution to this problem is to rewrite the log methods in the Init servlet (as discussed in Chapter 4's section "Configuration and Initialization") to implement the new logging mechanism. The drawback of that is some code might legitimately use log methods of servlets' interface directly (see, for example, Listing 5.9), and for such code our changes to Init servlet will not have any effect.

Please note that while logging itself is a legitimate crosscutting concern (as discussed in Chapter 6), the logging mechanism is not. The logging mechanism is just a method that provides some limited localized functionality, in this case, writing out log records. But when faced with changing it, the logging method suddenly starts exhibiting crosscutting behavior caused by the widespread use of its interfaces throughout the program. Or, more precisely, it is our problem that becomes crosscutting, not really the method per se.

The problem can be formulated so that the logging has to be changed to use the new method (whatever it is, we are not going to dwell on it) in all places that use servlet API calls for it. As you have noticed, the problem is about "places," not the "method." As a matter of fact, the Init servlet's log methods are just such places; the servlet does not really implement any logging mechanism on its own, but uses servlet's container. Because the correct problem definition represents 50% of the solution, the solution is easy to suggest: Find all the places that use servlet logging and replace them. It leads to the aspect in Listing 8.1.

LISTING 8.1   NewLogging.java Aspect

```
package aspects;

import javax.servlet.*;

public aspect NewLogging
{
    void around(String message) :
    (
        call(void GenericServlet.log(String))
        ||
        call(void ServletContext.log(String))
    )
    && args(message)
    {
        System.out.println(message);
    }

    void around(String message, Throwable ex) :
    (
        call(void GenericServlet.log(String, Throwable))
        ||
        call(void ServletContext.log(String, Throwable))
    )
    && args(message, ex)
    {
        System.out.println(message);
        ex.printStackTrace(System.out);
    }
}
```

The implementation of this aspect calls for finding and replacing all calls to the log() methods. The servlet API provides for two ways of calling the log: one in

GenericServlet class, another in ServletContext. The AspectNews application uses both (one in Register servlet, another in Init), so we have to write the appropriate pointcuts. Two around advices are necessary because two different signatures of the log() methods have to be exposed. For the sake of simplicity, we emulate the new logging mechanism by calling standard output methods for strings and exceptions.

It is worth emphasizing that the crosscutting concern in this situation is not the logging method, but rather the necessity of finding and correcting all uses of it.

New Levels of Service

As an example of a realistic business scenario, let's consider this idea: The news service has to be expanded and now users will get charged for the content. This represents several problems. First, each story now has to have a price along with all that goes with it, that is, access methods, persistence, and so on. Second, we need some way to track usage, and then bill for it. It is possible either to implement new versions of the Story class (see Listing 4.5) and the StoriesDb.retrieve() method (see Listing 4.11), or encapsulate the new functionality as an aspect (see Listing 8.2).

LISTING 8.2 PaidStories.java Aspect

```
package aspects;

import db.*;
import java.util.*;

public aspect PaidStories
{
    private double Story.price = 0;

    public void Story.setPrice(double price)
    {
        this.price = price;
    }

    public double Story.getPrice()
    {
        return price;
    }

    pointcut billThem(String user):
      call(Collection StoriesDb.retrieve(String)) && args(user);
```

LISTING 8.2   Continued

```
Collection around(String user) : billThem(user)
{
    Collection stories = proceed(user);

    for(Iterator i=stories.iterator(); i.hasNext(); )
    {
        Story story = (Story)i.next();
        chargeUser(user, story.getPrice());
    }

    return stories;
}

private void chargeUser(String user, double price)
{
    // implementation goes here
}
}
```

The aspect does two things. It introduces one more field, `price`, to the `Story` object, and two more methods to set and get it. Note that we have skipped the persistence issues for clarity. The pointcut `billThem()` picks calls to `StoriesDb.retrieve()` method and triggers the corresponding `around()` advice that calculates the total price of all retrieved stories, and then charges the user (whose ID is obtained as an advice parameter) using the unimplemented method `chargeUser()`. It is straightforward enough.

Now, let's consider a not so straightforward issue: Is it a good idea? From one point of view, billing is a crosscutting concern if considered in the context described in Part I of this book. From another, we just used AspectJ to implement a new feature with relatively limited crosscutting scope—only two classes were involved and there were other means of "cleanly" developing the same functionality. From the third point of view (keep counting, please), a traditional approach would entail a whole new iteration of a development cycle including design, development, testing, release, and so on.

The previously described aspect (this is the forth point) is just a small patch that contains only the required functionality and does not touch the core system. The system will work with or without it, so only this little aspect needs to be released. Yet another argument can be made about the effect that constant patching will have on the system's overall structure. It would be impossible to tell what the application is supposed to do by looking at the original source code because all immediately apparent functionality will be heavily advised and, thus, amended. It compares unfavorably to patching a piece of code in place where the result stays in the same file. A good counterargument to this is that nobody can tell much from looking at an individual class source, anyway; it is all meaningless outside the overall class structure with all its numerous diagrams, design documents, use cases, and so on. This arsenal of auxiliary tools and theories has not yet been developed for aspect-oriented programming and, perhaps, this is the problem.

Or, returning to the point briefly discussed in Chapter 7's section "Caching," is it good practice to use aspects for something not that aspect-oriented? Because there is still very limited amount of commonly accepted usage patterns for aspect-oriented systems, the answer depends on your point of view. You can pick one of about eight described in the previous paragraph or have your own. This is not to say that accepted patterns or points of view should dictate your decision, but some help certainly would not hurt—it is not there yet and you are on your own.

Maybe, just maybe, we are on the verge of a paradigm shift (yes, think outside the box or pick another management cliché of your choice), which will lead to a new aspect-based development methodology? This methodology would enable us to construct programs starting with a core class structure plus a chain of various aspects that modify core behavior until the result fits the specification. Only time will tell.

Summary

In this chapter we see that aspects are really helpful in adapting the AspectNews application to the changing world. Taking this adaptation idea a little further allows us to explore (or, more precisely, to start exploring) a possibility of devising an aspect-based development methodology.

9

Transition to Deployment

IN THIS CHAPTER

- Catalog of Aspects
- Performance of the Aspects
- Documentation and Packaging

In this chapter we will discuss the AspectNews application's runtime properties and decide what goes into the distribution. Some packaging techniques will also be described.

Catalog of Aspects

We have developed aspects of three main kinds:

- Aspects that AspectNews application can do without are called *development aspects*. These aspects can be used as development aids, but they are of limited utility beyond that.

- Aspects that are absolutely essential to the application are called *production aspects*. This means that the application simply will not function without them.

- Aspects that are useful, but not critical are called *runtime aspects*. The application is better off with them than without.

The previous classifications lead to the breakdown of aspects shown in Table 9.1.

TABLE 9.1   Aspects of the AspectNews Application

Kind	Aspect	Description
Development	Logger and its derivatives	Logs messages at join points.
	Profiler	Creates an execution profile.
	Tracer	Traces execution path.
	CodeSegregation	Issues warnings and errors about misplaced database code.
Production	Authentication	Implements security functionality.
	Exceptions	Simplifies exception handling.
	NullChecker	Enforces "not null" interface contract.
Runtime	Pooling	Pools database connections.
	ConnectionChecking	Checks database connections.
	ReadCache	Implements caching of the news stories.
	OutputStreamBuffering	Implements data buffering.

The aspects developed in Chapter 8, "Coping with Change," are just examples of addressing the future problems and, at the moment, are not required for AspectNews.

Obviously, the development aspects do not need to be compiled into the production version of the application—their sole purpose was to assist in development. It is also obvious, that production aspects cannot be excluded because application will not work without them. However, the runtime aspects are subject of the separate discussion.

Performance of the Aspects

We do not intend to prove obvious facts that caching, pooling, and buffering increase performance. Our problem is what practical effect all these wonderful things will have on this particular application. Luckily, we have a tool to use in our experiments—the Profiler aspect described in detail in Chapter 6, "Development Aids."

Let's conduct an unscientific "stress test" of the application according to the following scenario:

1. A user logs in.

2. The user retrieves his stories five times in a row.

3. The user deselects one of his story categories.

4. The user retrieves his stories five times in a row.

5. The user reselects one of his story categories.

6. The user retrieves his stories five times in a row.

7. The user submits a new story.

8. The user retrieves his stories five times in a row.

This sequence of events will be repeated for another user from another browser session, and then the whole exercise will be repeated again for both users with a different application build.

We will need two versions of the application built for the test: one with runtime aspects compiled in, another without. To simplify the task of building and rebuilding the application with different sets of aspects, we will modify the `exclude` macro in the `build.properties` file (see Listing 3.1 for the full source), as shown in Listing 9.1.

LISTING 9.1   Groupings of Aspects in the `build.properties` File

```
# Various groups of aspects
developmentAspects=aspects/Logger.java,aspects/Logger1.java,\
aspects/Logger2.java,aspects/Tracer.java,aspects/CodeSegregation.java
runtimeAspects=aspects/Pooling.java,aspects/ConnectionChecking.java,\
aspects/ReadCache.java,aspects/OutputStreamBuffering.java
changeAspects=aspects/NewLogging.java,aspects/PaidStories.java

# All core AspectNews aspects
#exclude=${changeAspects}

# No development aspects
exclude=${changeAspects},${developmentAspects}

# No development or runtime aspects
#exclude=${changeAspects},${developmentAspects},${runtimeAspects}
```

All the aspects we have developed are grouped in four categories: three as described in Table 9.1 and aspects that reflect future changes. The latter category is always excluded, the production aspects are never excluded, which leaves us with three choices for the build: application with all aspects compiled in, with development aspects excluded, and with development and runtime aspects excluded. For the performance exercise, we are interested in the last two possibilities; the `Profiler` aspect must not be excluded, of course.

The results of the "stress test" analyzed by our crude profiler tool are shown in Table 9.2. Column 1 corresponds to the build without runtime aspects; 2, with runtime aspects; 3, same as 2, but with the `NullChecker` aspect excluded. Subcolumns marked *a* contain the number of method invocations; those marked *b* indicate the average time spent in the corresponding method in milliseconds.

TABLE 9.2 Profiler Results

1		2		3		Methods
a	b	a	b	a	b	
610	0.16	640	0.14	670	0.15	BodyContent javax.servlet.jsp.tagext. BodyTagSupport. getBodyContent()
702	0.13	732	0.10	762	0.13	boolean java.sql.ResultSet.next()
648	0.09	678	0.12	708	0.08	boolean java.util.Collection.add (Object)
666	0.17	696	0.06	726	0.19	boolean java.util.Iterator.hasNext()
40	2.00	40	0.50	40	0.25	Collection db.StoriesDb.retrieve (String)
60	24.20	1	311.00	1	171.00	Connection java.sql.DriverManager. getConnection(String, String, String)
128	0.09	128	0.16	128	0.00	HttpSession javax.servlet.jsp. PageContext.getSession()
18	14.44	18	1.11	18	0.56	int java.sql.Statement. executeUpdate(String)
44	0.23	44	0.23	44	0.00	Iterator java.util.Collection. iterator()
610	0.10	640	0.16	672	0.25	JspWriter javax.servlet.jsp.tagext. BodyTagSupport. getPreviousOut()
622	0.06	652	0.05	682	0.26	Object java.util.Iterator.next()
134	2.54	134	0.07	134	0.22	Object javax.servlet.http. HttpSession. getAttribute(String)

TABLE 9.2   Continued

1		2		3		Methods
a	b	a	b	a	b	
64	0.00	64	0.00	64	0.31	`Object org.aspectj.lang.JoinPoint. getTarget()`
40	0.25	40	0.25	40	0.25	`PageContext security.BodyTagSupport. getPageContext()`
54	0.74	54	2.96	54	6.67	`ResultSet java.sql.Statement. executeQuery(String)`
1260	0.11	1320	0.12	1380	0.16	`String java.sql.ResultSet.getString (int)`
		2	5.00	2	0.00	`String javax.servlet.jsp.tagext. TagData.getAttributeString (String)`
185	0.11	185	0.11	185	0.11	`String javax.servlet.ServletContext .getInitParameter(String))`
8	0.00	8	1.25	8	3.75	`String javax.servlet.ServletRequest .getParameter(String)`
185	0.34	185	0.32	185	0.22	`String servlets.Init.getParameter (String)`
60	1.00					`void java.sql.Connection.close()`
22	0.00	22	0.91	22	0.45	`void javax.servlet.jsp.JspWriter. print(String)`
610	0.21	640	0.14	670	0.18	`void javax.servlet.jsp. PageContext.setAttribute (String, Object)`
610	0.23	640	0.06	672	0.28	`void javax.servlet.jsp.tagext. BodyContent.clearBody()`

TABLE 9.2   Continued

1	2	3				Methods
a	b	a	b	a	b	
610	0.21	640	0.13	672	0.10	void javax.servlet.jsp. tagext.BodyContent. writeOut(Writer)
68	0.59	68	0.29	4	7.50	void javax.servlet.ServletContext .log(String)
4	7.50	4	2.50	4	7.50	void servlets.Init.log(String)

Methods invoked only once (for example, Class
java.lang.Class.forName(String)) and methods with zero execution time (such as
JspWriter javax.servlet.jsp.PageContext.getOut()) are dropped from the result
set to avoid clutter.

As expected, the runtime aspects saved a lot of execution time. For example, without
Pooling aspect the program spent 60×24.2=1452ms trying to establish connections
to the database 60 times in a row. On the other hand, with Pooling, only one
connection was established and it took between 171 and 311ms (see the row with
DriverManager.getConnection() method). During our tests, the
db.StoriesDb.retrieve() method—the workhorse of the entire application—was
called 40 times and it took 40×2.0=80ms without ReadCache aspect—with the aspect
performance increased four fold: 0.50ms per call versus 2.00ms.

The aspect NullChecker is classified as a production aspect (see Table 9.1) because its
purpose is contract enforcement; it is there by design, so to speak. At the same time,
it is quite obvious that it would be an extremely rare runtime event if a null object is
passed to any of the database methods. The NullChecker aspect adds one method
call on every database operation and during this call its arguments have to be
obtained and iterated over to be checked. It sounds like a lot of overhead, but is it
enough to be concerned? It is easy to verify, the aspect just needs to be added to the
list of classes to exclude from compilation in the build.properties file:

```
exclude=${changeAspects},${developmentAspects},aspects/NullChecker.java
```

Results of profiling are in column 3 of Table 9.2. Although almost all methods show
similar execution time (column 2 contains the same build plus the NullChecker), the
results for db.StoriesDb.retrieve() method have improved again: 0.25ms versus

0.50ms per call. Again, the result is obvious—more overhead slows things down, but the degree of the performance impact needs to be considered. Will we tolerate an occasional `NullPointerException` in exchange for twice the speed? And if the application is thoroughly tested, how occasional is occasional? What will happen if the `NullPointerException` is thrown? All these issues quickly become a judgment call for the designer—performance versus reliability is an age-old compromise. Luckily, we have the tools to analyze them.

Another practical runtime consideration is what aspects advise what classes (or another aspects). In the AspectNews application, the `OutputStreamBuffering` aspect works its magic on instances of `FileOutputStream` class. It so happens that the only place where these streams are used is the `Profiler` aspect, which is, by design, a development aid. Because there is no need to include the `Profiler` aspect into the runtime distribution, the `OutputStreamBuffering` aspect should not be included either, unless there are other instances of `FileOutputStream` class that you want to advise.

Documentation and Packaging

The only thing left to do with the AspectNews application is to pack up and go. Because AspectNews is a Web application, its packaging rules are governed by the servlet specification (for specification details, see Appendix F, "References"). But this refers only to the "executable" part of it. We also have to provide some form of documentation to go along.

Luckily, the AspectJ distribution includes a tool called `ajdoc` that extends the standard `javadoc` functionality to support aspects and aspect-related extensions to Java syntax (see Appendix B, "AspectJ Command-Line Tools," for details). There is also a corresponding Ant task to call on it.

But let's do it in an orderly fashion and modify AspectNews's `build.xml` file to support distribution and documentation building. First, we need to define a special `ajdoc` task to invoke the doc generator from Ant:

```
<taskdef name="ajdoc"
    classname="org.aspectj.tools.ant.taskdefs.Ajdoc" >
    <classpath>
      <pathelement location="${aspectj}/aspectj-ant.jar"/>
      <pathelement location="${aspectj}lib/aspectjtools.jar"/>
    </classpath>
  </taskdef>
```

Second, we need to define a distribution target:

```
<target name="dist" depends="deploy">
  <!-- Create the distribution directory -->
  <mkdir dir="${dist}"/>
  <mkdir dir="${dist}/doc"/>

  <jar jarfile="${dist}/${app.name}.war" basedir="${deploy}"/>

  <!-- this task is still in development
  <ajdoc srcdir="${src}"
         destdir="${dist}/doc"
         packagenames="tags/*,security/*,servlets/*,db/*,common/*,aspects/*"
  >
    <classpath>
      <pathelement location="${aspectj}lib/aspectjrt.jar"/>
      <pathelement location="${catalina}/common/lib/servlet.jar"/>
    </classpath>
  </ajdoc>
  -->

  <!-- "Manual" replacement of the ajdoc task -->
  <exec dir="${src}" executable="${aspectj}bin/ajdoc.bat" vmlauncher="false">
    <arg line="-classpath ${aspectj}lib/aspectjrt.jar;
        ${aspectj}lib/aspectjtools.jar;${catalina}/common/lib/servlet.jar"/>
    <arg line="-d ../${dist}/doc"/>
    <arg line="aspects/*.java db/*java security/*.java tags/*java
                                                servlets/*java"/>
  </exec>

</target>
```

This target depends on the `deploy` target, and it packs the content of the Tomcat's Web application directory into an `AspectNews.war` archive. Ant conveniently provides a `jar` task to accomplish this. The archive contains everything you need to deploy the AspectNews application in the servlet container of choice including the AspectJ runtime library and MySQL's JDBC driver (make sure that your distribution contains only the components you are legally allowed to redistribute).

In Tomcat's case, the `AspectNews.war` application can be deployed either by using the Tomcat's `manager` application or by including the following context into `server.xml` configuration file:

```
<Context path="/AspectNews" docBase="AspectNews.war"
                                        reloadable="true" debug="0">
   <Logger className="org.apache.catalina.logger.FileLogger"
      prefix="aspectnews." suffix=".log" timestamp="true"/>
</Context>
```

The server has to be restarted for the changes to take effect.

In addition to the regular content of the documentation produced by Java, the files have several especially handy features. Each file generated for an aspect (see Figure 9.1) contains the following:

- Fully explained instantiation declaration (singleton versus per target versus per this, and so on).

- List of known advices, which is extremely helpful for debugging.

- All aspect-specific declarations such as introductions and lists of advices with the enumeration of all the methods they affect.

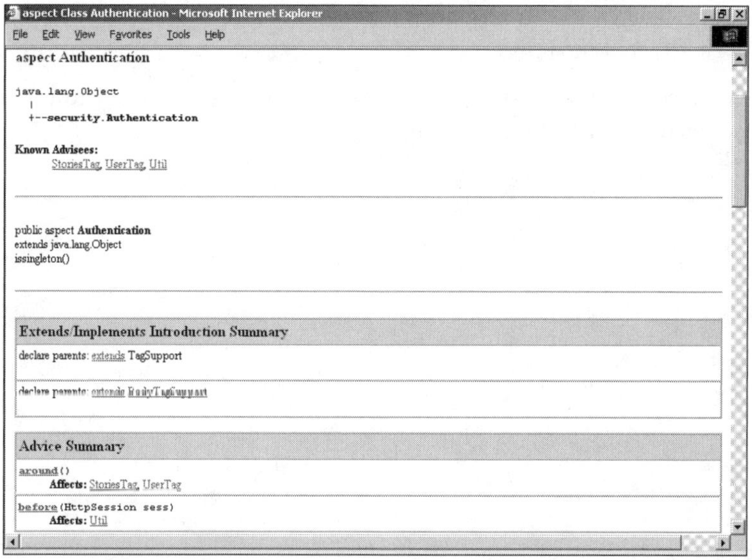

FIGURE 9.1 An example of the `ajdoc`-generated documentation: Authentication aspect.

All these files will be generated in the dist/doc directory and will not have to be included in the application archive AspectNews.war unless the development documentation will be considered a part of the application that should be available to the users.

The content of the `dist` directory is the AspectNews's distribution, and as such can be copied on CD or archived into a downloadable file.

Note: Unfortunately, at the time of this writing, the `ajdoc` task was still under development and had to be commented out of the distribution task. It was replaced with the "manual" version, that is, with the invocation of a command-line tool that produced the same result (we lost platform independence, though). It generated a set of HTML files similar to the regular javadoc's pages that contained documentation for the classes and aspects written for AspectNews application. Figure 9.1 showed an example of the output.

Summary

This chapter is the end of the extended example exploring the uses of AspectJ. As in any example, some parts of it are somewhat contrived, but it's important to keep in mind that not all the tool's features can be demonstrated in the context of a single application. The goal was to provide a look and feel for aspect-oriented programming and the AspectJ tool in action.

The next part of the book will give more details on the language features, especially those that were not used in this example.

PART III

Language Details

IN THIS PART

In a logically perfect language, there will be one word and no more for every simple object, and everything that is not simple will be expressed by a combination of words, by a combination derived, of course, from the words for the simple things that enter in, one word for each simple component.

—Bertrand Russell, *Logic and Knowledge*, "The Philosophy of Logical Atomism"

In this part of the book, we will examine AspectJ language in detail. The goal is to illustrate each particular feature of the language with a brief, but meaningful example—no matter how contrived—with compactness as a major concern. All examples should be compiled and executed from the command line, as described in Part I, no specific build file is provided. The detailed instructions are given as needed.

10

Aspects

IN THIS CHAPTER

- Extension
- Instantiation
- Domination

Aspects are major units of crosscutting implementations. They are similar to classes in many respects, but the most important difference is that aspects can crosscut types, that is, affect and modify other classes. The similarities and differences of aspects and regular Java classes are summarized in the Table 10.1.

TABLE 10.1 Comparison of Aspects and Classes

Feature	Classes	Aspects
Can be directly instantiated	yes	no
Can extend classes	yes	yes
Can implement interfaces	yes	yes
Can extend aspects	no	yes[1]
Can be declared inner	yes	yes[2]

1 Only abstract aspects can be extended
2 Must also be declared static

As you saw in Part I, the AspectJ compiler translates aspects into Java classes, so certain caution should be exercised. For example, it would be a mistake to define an aspect and a class with the same name in the same package (filenames, obviously, have to be different anyway).

Let's discuss aspect features one by one.

Extension

An example of peculiarity of aspects is their *extension*, wherein rules are different for traditional Java items (classes, methods, fields) than they are for AspectJ's

(aspects, pointcuts, advices). AspectJ takes a minimalist stand on inheritance functionality, but it affords interesting possibilities nevertheless.

Consider the following example:

```
public abstract aspect Parent
{
    abstract pointcut a();

    void a()
    {
        System.out.println("Parent's a");
    }

    before(): a()
    {
        System.out.println("Parent's before "+thisJoinPoint.getKind());
    }
}
```

The `Parent` aspect is declared abstract and contains an abstract pointcut `a()`, a
`before()` advice that is triggered by it, and a method `void a()`. The advice prints out
its identification along with the kind of join point it runs on to help us to find out
what pointcut caused its execution.

The `Child` aspect extends `Parent` and is also declared abstract. It adds concrete pointcuts `a()` and `b()`, and a method `void b()`:

```
public abstract aspect Child extends Parent
{
    pointcut a(): execution(* *.test());
    pointcut b(): call(* *.test());

    void b()
    {
        System.out.println("Child's b");
    }
}
```

Implementing pointcut `a()` overrides the abstract declaration and makes `Parent`'s
`before()` advice run if the pointcut picks any join points (it will).

The third aspect, `GrandChild`, is concrete. It also implements pointcut `a()` from
aspect `Parent` and, in addition, has a method `void c()` and a `before()` advice triggered by the `b()` pointcut inherited from the `Child` aspect:

```
public aspect GrandChild extends Child
{
    pointcut a(): call(* *.test());

    void c()
    {
        System.out.println("GrandChild's c");
    }

    before(): b()
    {
        System.out.println("GrandChild's before");
    }
}
```

These are examples of primitive pointcuts that pick calls to a method test() of whatever class or its execution.

The Inheritance class just provides such a method to be advised along with the main() method:

```
public class Inheritance
{
    public static final String cvs="$Id$";

    void test()
    {
        System.out.println("Inside method test");
    }

    public static void main(String args[])
    {
        try
        {
            GrandChild asp = GrandChild.aspectOf();

            asp.a();
            asp.b();
            asp.c();

            Inheritance inh = new Inheritance();
            inh.test();
        }
```

```
        catch(Throwable t)
        {
            System.out.println("Exception in main:"+t);
            t.printStackTrace(System.out);
        }
    }
}
```

The whole example can be compiled using the following command:

```
>ajc Parent.java Child.java GrandChild.java Inheritance.java
```

and run by issuing

```
>java Inheritance
```

It produces the following output:

```
Parent's a
Child's b
GrandChild's c
GrandChild's before
Parent's before method-call
Inside method test
```

Inside the `Inheritance.main()` method the following things are happening: First, an instance of the `GrandChild` aspect is obtained using the static `GrandChild.aspectOf()` method. This method is generated by the AspectJ compiler and returns a statically constructed instance of the Java class that corresponds to a translated aspect. The aspect instance returned behaves just like a regular instance of a Java class—because it is. Namely, instance and class methods can be invoked on it. Methods `Parent.a()` and `Child.b()` were successfully inherited from the parent abstract aspects as they would be in the case of regular Java classes. It is, of course, no surprise that abstract aspects translate to abstract classes, hence the similarity in behavior.

Second, an instance of the `Inheritance` class is explicitly created, and the `test()` method is called, thus giving an opportunity for the advices to run. The `GrandChild`'s before advice is triggered by the `Child`'s `b()` pointcut. Nothing prevents an abstract aspect to define a concrete pointcut, and as seen in the code, it can be inherited and used in derivative aspects. The same is true for an abstract pointcut: `Parent`'s `a()` pointcut was implemented twice (in `Child` and `GrandChild` aspects), but which one was in effect? Judging by the output, it was `GrandChild`'s—it is a call pointcut, `Child`'s one is an execution. If you comment out the `a()` pointcut in

GrandChild aspect, compilation and execution of the example will produce the following:

```
Parent's a
Child's b
GrandChild's c
GrandChild's before
Parent's before method-execution
Inside method test
```

This means, the Parent's before() advice was triggered on execution join point picked by Child's a() pointcut. In other words, pointcuts can be implemented and overridden pretty much as regular Java instance methods—abstract and otherwise. In this case, though, the similarity in behavior is superficial—pointcuts have nothing to do with methods per se.

Instantiation

As we discussed before, aspects cannot be manually instantiated; that is, you cannot invoke the new() operator on them, clone them, or use serialization to create them. At most, an aspect can have a constructor that cannot take any arguments or throw any nonruntime exceptions. It all sounds overly restrictive, but it's for the better because an advice needs an aspect instance to run, and the AspectJ compiler can make very smart decisions when and how one can be created. In the next several sections we will discuss available instantiation methods and what they can do.

For illustration purposes we will need a couple of Java classes that will be advised by our forthcoming instantiation examples.

The Test.java class is as follows:

```
public class Test
{
    public void test()
    {
    }
}
```

And here's the Instantiation.java class:

```
public class Instantiation
{
    public static Test st = new Test();
```

```
    public void run()
    {
        st.test();

        Test t = new Test();
        t.test();
    }

    public static void main(String args[])
    {
        try
        {
            System.out.println("This:          Target:          Aspect:");
            for(int i=0; i<3; i++)
            {
                (new Instantiation()).run();
            }
        }
        catch(Throwable t)
        {
            System.out.println("Exception in main:"+t);
            t.printStackTrace(System.out);
        }
    }
}
```

The Instantiation class does not do anything useful, but create instances of Test and Instantiation objects. Its main() method starts by printing the header for the future aspect's output (you will see an example later), and then proceeds to create three instances of the Instantiation object and call its run() method. This method, in turn, calls the test() method of the static instance of a Test object st, and then creates a new instance of Test and calls its test() method again. To summarize, this little program creates three instances of class Instantiation, four instances of class Test (one of them static), and calls Test.test() six times (three of them on static instance). In the next section it will become apparent why we went to all this trouble.

Singletons

By definition, an aspect inherits the instantiation policy from its parent or it is implicitly singleton; that is, AspectJ will create one instance of it for the lifetime of the program.

The keyword issingleton can be either explicitly mentioned in the aspect declaration as in the following Singleton.java aspect example or omitted:

```
public aspect Singleton issingleton()
{
    pointcut a() : call(* *.test()) && this(Instantiation);

    before(): a()
    {
        System.out.println(
            "  "+thisJoinPoint.getThis()+
            "  "+thisJoinPoint.getTarget()+
            "  "+Singleton.aspectOf());
    }
}
```

The aspect's a() pointcut picks calls to method test() and also captures a reference to currently executing objects by using the this() primitive pointcut (see Chapter 11, "Picking Join Points: Pointcuts," for details). The before() advice triggered by the a() pointcut prints references to this (currently executing), target (to be advised), and aspect objects.

The following command can be used to compile the aspect with the classes it needs to advise:

```
>ajc Instantiation.java Test.java Singleton.java
```

When executed, the Instantiation program thus advised produces the following output:

```
This:                   Target:       Aspect:
Instantiation@169e11    Test@639a3e   Singleton@239137
Instantiation@169e11    Test@12e78c   Singleton@239137
Instantiation@1fbe93    Test@639a3e   Singleton@239137
Instantiation@1fbe93    Test@18dfaf   Singleton@239137
Instantiation@58610     Test@639a3e   Singleton@239137
Instantiation@58610     Test@2498b5   Singleton@239137
```

As expected, there are three instances of the this object (class Instantiation with hash codes 0x169e11, 0x1fbe93, and 0x58610, respectively). There are also four instances of the target object (the object whose methods were affected by the advise, in this case—Test class with hash codes 0x639a3e (the static one), 0x12e78c, 0x18dfaf, and 0x2498b5). And in all six calls to Test.test() method picked by Singleton's a() pointcut, only one instance of the Singleton aspect was in existence—the one with the hash code 0x239137.

It is easy to see how the AspectJ compiler implements a singleton aspect by looking at the generated code. The compiled `Singleton` aspect (edited for brevity) is as follows:

```
public class Singleton
{
  ...
  public static Singleton aspect$;
  public static Singleton aspectOf()
  {
    return Singleton.aspect$;
  }
  ...
  static
  {
    Singleton.aspect$ = new Singleton();
  }
}
```

Indeed, there is one statically created static instance of the aspect and it is kept in the aspect$ class variable. The instance can be obtained by calling the `Singleton.aspectOf()` static method. The singularity of the aspect is, therefore, guaranteed by the virtue of the static initialization. Here lies the root of aspects' crosscutting properties.

PerThis **Aspects**

As was shown in Chapter 7, sometimes the singularity of aspects' instances is an impediment rather than a benefit. AspectJ allows several additional instantiation options to accommodate such situations.

Let's begin with the `perthis` definition. If an aspect is declared with a `perthis(poincut)` qualifier, an instance of it is created for each target picked by the pointcut in the declaration. Consider a version of a previously described `Singleton` aspect modified with the `perthis` declaration:

```
public aspect PerThis perthis(a())
{
    pointcut a() : call(* *.test()) && this(Instantiation);

    before(): a()
    {
        System.out.println(
            "  "+thisJoinPoint.getThis()+
            "  "+thisJoinPoint.getTarget()+
```

```
        "  "+PerThis.aspectOf(thisJoinPoint.getThis()));
    }
}
```

An instance of this aspect will be created for each instance of the currently executing object (of class Instantiation in this example). If compiled and executed along with Instantiation and Test classes, the following output results:

```
This:                  Target:        Aspect:
Instantiation@239137   Test@12e78c    PerThis@1fbe93
Instantiation@239137   Test@18dfaf    PerThis@1fbe93
Instantiation@58610    Test@12e78c    PerThis@2498b5
Instantiation@58610    Test@25ab41    PerThis@2498b5
Instantiation@e3e60    Test@12e78c    PerThis@2125f0
Instantiation@e3e60    Test@41cd1f    PerThis@2125f0
```

As you can see, for each of the three instances of the Instantiation object a new PerThis aspect was created, their respective hash codes form one-to-one relationship:

```
Instantiation -> PerThis
239137        -> 1fbe93
58610         -> 2498b5
e3e60         -> 2125f0
```

The mechanics of perthis implementation is rather complicated to discuss in detail here, but there is still no magic. The PerThis class defines an inner interface AJC_HasAspect that has to be implemented by all affected this classes—in our case, by the compiled Instantiation object. The interface contains all methods for associating aspects to object instances, and the AspectJ compiler conveniently generates them all (browsing generated code can be truly revelational at times).

NOTE

Please note that there is no longer an aspectOf() method because there is no single aspect. A replacement method is provided that takes an object argument and returns the aspect associated with that object, if any. A runtime exception org.aspectj.lang.NoAspectBoundException is thrown if there is no such association. Because this is a perthis aspect, the current join point's getThis() method returns just the object.

PerTarget **Aspects**

PerTarget aspects are similar to perthis in intentions and implementation details. The major difference is that an aspect is created per target object of the declared pointcut—that is, the object whose method is affected by the aspect's advice. Here is the example of such aspect:

```
public aspect PerTarget pertarget(a())
{
    pointcut a() : call(* *.test()) && this(Instantiation);

    before(): a()
    {
        System.out.println(
            "  "+thisJoinPoint.getThis()+
            "  "+thisJoinPoint.getTarget()+
            "  "+PerTarget.aspectOf(thisJoinPoint.getTarget()));
    }
}
```

When compiled and executed, as in the previous example, it produces the following output:

```
This:                 Target:     Aspect:
Instantiation@239137  Test@12e78c PerTarget@1fbe93
Instantiation@239137  Test@18dfaf PerTarget@58610
Instantiation@2498b5  Test@12e78c PerTarget@1fbe93
Instantiation@2498b5  Test@25ab41 PerTarget@e3e60
Instantiation@2125f0  Test@12e78c PerTarget@1fbe93
Instantiation@2125f0  Test@41cd1f PerTarget@1afa3
```

Because the `Instantiation` class creates four instances of the target object `Test`, four `PerTarget` aspects are indeed created:

```
Test    -> PerTarget
12e78c -> 1fbe93 (this is the static one)
18dfaf -> 58610
25ab41 -> e3e60
41cd1f -> 1afa3
```

As is the case with the `perthis` aspects, the `aspectOf()` method has to receive an object parameter, but in this case a target for which the aspect was created.

Per-Control-Flow Aspects

The most dynamic option of aspect instantiation is `percflow`—an aspect is created every time the execution enters a control flow picked by the declared pointcut. (A variant of it, `percflowbelow` does the same thing, but below the flow will be discussed in Chapter 12, "Advices.")

Here is the familiar aspect again:

```
public aspect PerCflow percflow(a())
{
    pointcut a() : call(* *.test()) && this(Instantiation);

    before(): a()
    {
        System.out.println(
            "  "+thisJoinPoint.getThis()+
            "  "+thisJoinPoint.getTarget()+
            "  "+PerCflow.aspectOf());
    }
}
```

Because pointcut a() picks calls to the Test.test() method, and there are six such calls made in the course of Instantiation class execution, six instances of PerCflow aspect are expected to be created—one per execution path (control flow):

This:	Target:	Aspect:
Instantiation@1fbe93	Test@18dfaf	PerCflow@58610
Instantiation@1fbe93	Test@2498b5	PerCflow@25ab41
Instantiation@e3e60	Test@18dfaf	PerCflow@2125f0
Instantiation@e3e60	Test@41cd1f	PerCflow@1afa3
Instantiation@31f71a	Test@18dfaf	PerCflow@5601ea
Instantiation@31f71a	Test@17d257	PerCflow@7259da

As in previous examples for issingleton, perthis, and pertarget aspects, there are three Instantiation object instances and four Test instances, but the aspects for each invocation of Test.test() are all different.

The aspectOf() method does not need any parameters in the case of percflow aspects because when it is called, the control flow is always current. That is, if an aspect was created for it, one is available—in the case of multithreaded execution, it does not matter which particular one.

Internally, AspectJ runtime keeps a stack of percflow aspects. They are created as soon as control flow is entered, and destroyed (in the Java meaning of the word) as soon as it has left. During the execution, the aspects are dispensed from the stack as needed by peeking into it, and thus, the correct count is maintained. Obviously, if an elaborate aspect is designed, its construction on each execution flow might get pretty taxing—as it would be with any Java class of similar complexity plus AspectJ's runtime overhead.

Domination

As you saw in Chapter 7, "Runtime Improvements," the order in which aspects are applied is not defined by default. AspectJ provides a special syntax that enables you to change application priority—the whole concept is called *domination*. If an aspect A is declared to dominate another aspect B, it means that the advices of A have more priority than the advices of B. For related aspects, the implicit rule is that the child dominates the parent.

To discuss details, let's consider an example. Here is a simple (as simple as it gets) Domination.java class that will be advised:

```
public class Domination
{
    public static void main(String args[])
    {
        // nothing
    }
}
```

Now assume we have four absolutely identical aspects (they differ only in their names, DominationA, DominationB, DominationC, and DominationD, so only the first one is shown here):

```
public aspect DominationA
{
    before(): execution(public static void Domination.main(..))
    {
        System.out.println(this.getClass().getName());
    }
}
```

The aspects execute their before() advices when Domination.main() method is about to run. The advices print out the corresponding aspect's name. Note, that this in the code has nothing to do with the join point's this object. It is Java's literal reference to the current object, that is, the object the aspect will be translated to, not the object picked by the pointcut at the join point and obtained by calling thisJoinPoint.getThis() method.

The example can be compiled and executed as follows:

```
>ajc Domination*.java
>java Domination
```

It will produce the following output:

```
DominationA
DominationB
DominationC
DominationD
```

The order of advice application looks alphabetic by aspect name, but compared to our unexpressed intentions (well, maybe we wanted it in reverse) it is as good as random—and for all practical purposes, it is.

The `dominates` keyword increases the precedence of one aspect over another (or several others—see the following). Let's change the declaration of `DominationC` aspect to

```
public aspect DominationC dominates DominationA
```

Compiling and running the example produces

```
DominationB
DominationC
DominationA
DominationD
```

That is, with all other things being equally random, the `DominationC` advice runs before that of `DominationA`.

The domination syntax enables you to use type patterns in the definition of dominated aspects. Let's declare `DominationD` to dominate everything else (in this example, every aspects whose name begins with `Dom`):

```
public aspect DominationD dominates Dom*
```

It produces the following:

```
DominationD
DominationB
DominationC
DominationA
```

`DominationD`'s advice runs before anything else and `DominationC`'s before `DominationA`'s.

What if a domination declaration creates a conflict situation? For example, what if we declare `DominationA` and `DominationB` to dominate each other:

```
public aspect DominationB dominates DominationA
public aspect DominationA dominates DominationB
```

Unfortunately, the compiler just ignores the problem. The example compiles and runs just fine producing the output presented previously.

Summary

In this chapter we described the major component of AspectJ: an aspect. It is in many ways similar to a Java class, but in addition AspectJ provides more features to fine-tune the instantiation and crosscutting behavior. The next chapter will describe pointcuts—the things that tell aspects what to crosscut.

11

Picking Join Points: Pointcuts

In this chapter we will discuss join points, pointcuts, and related language features; AspectJ has a whole sublanguage to describe the desired crosscuts of the code. We will examine type patterns, signatures, contexts, and other elements of it.

Join Points and Pointcuts

You are probably keenly aware that computers cannot read people's mind. The good news, for now at least, is that we still have some control over them. The bad news is that we have to be rather precise in telling them what to do. An application of the previous philosophical statement to the aspect-oriented programming means that the aspect tool (AspectJ in our case) must be instructed on what to crosscut. That is, as described in Chapter 1, "Why Aspect-Oriented Programming?" it needs these special markers in the code.

There are two choices: either insert the markers manually and let the tool find them, or make the tool create markers automatically as it goes, according to some language-specific convention. The first alternative defeats the purpose of crosscutting as an automation helper (modularization will still be happening). If a programmer has to touch sources to insert markers, he can also insert method (function) calls, and no additional tool is necessary. It all amounts to manual horizontal modularization (layering), which is already a popular programming technique. The second alternative, which is how AspectJ works, is much more innovative and productive.

As we have seen before, the AspectJ compiler can find places in the source code (or, in future versions, possibly the byte code) where some predefined (by Java) operation is executed: method calls, field assignments, and so on. These predefined operations, or well-defined points in program execution, are called join points.

AspectJ can possibly detect and operate on the following eleven kinds of join points:

- method call
- method execution
- constructor call
- initializer execution
- constructor execution
- static initializer execution
- object preinitialization
- object initialization
- field reference
- field assignment
- exception handler execution

The AspectJ language defines a syntactic construct to detect such join points, called a pointcut designator (PCD), or, simply, a pointcut. The difference between a join point and a pointcut is fundamental: The former is a concept, the latter is an AspectJ's language construct.

Pointcuts can be declared in aspects and classes and they behave like members; that is, they can be declared public, private, or final, but they cannot be overloaded. Pointcuts can also be declared abstract, but only inside abstract aspects. Pointcuts can be defined either named or nameless. A named pointcut's declaration should follow the following syntax:

```
pointcut Name(arguments): body;
```

Name is the pointcut's name that should comply with Java naming rules for identifiers. arguments is the list of arguments that should be exposed for the corresponding advices; it should follow the regular Java convention for the formal method parameters. The body contains the actual pointcut definition and can have either primitive pointcuts or a combination of other pointcuts (see the following). The nameless pointcuts contain just the body portion that must follow the advice declaration.

Primitive pointcuts have the following syntax:

```
kind(Signature|TypePattern|Identifier)
```

kind is the type of the pointcut (call, execution, and so forth). Signature is a method's or constructor's signature if the given pointcut requires it. TypePattern is a wild-card pattern that matches some Java types (again, if the given pointcut requires it). Finally, Identifier is Java's parameter name or pointcut name, depending on the context.

The syntax for the signature varies depending on the join point to be picked. Table 11.1 summarizes what should be included.

TABLE 11.1   Requirements for Signatures in Pointcuts

Join point	Type	Name	Parameters	Return value	Signature example
method call	of the object to be called on	of the method	of the method	of the method	Boolean Object. equals (Object)
method execution	of the corresponding class	of the method	of the method	of the method	Boolean Object.equals (Object)
constructor call	of the desired object		types of the constructor's parameters		String(byte[], int, int)
constructor execution	of the corresponding class		types of the constructor's parameters		String(byte[], int, int)
object initialization	of the initialized object		types of the first constructor's parameters		String(byte[], int, int)
object preinitialization	of the initialized object		types of the first constructor's parameters		String(byte[], int, int)
field reference or assignment	of the class the field belongs to, and the type of the field itself	of the field			int A.a
handler execution	of the exception				catch ClassCastException)

Wild Cards

In signature specifications wild cards are allowed: * matches any number of characters, and .. matches zero or more arguments. For example, the following means all methods returning double and accepting no arguments:

```
double *();
```

This will match all methods of class My that have last argument of a type String, return nothing, and their names begin with send:

```
void My.send*(.., String);
```

Similar pattern matching functionality is available for type patterns. * has its usual meaning—any number of characters (except a period [.]), but .. if used in type patterns (not in parameter lists of signatures) means any string that begins and ends with a period. This is very convenient for matching subpackages and inner types.

For example

```
javax.swing.plaf.*
```

will match any class in the javax.swing.plaf package, but not classes in any subpackages (such as javax.swing.plaf.metal), or inner classes of this package (such as javax.swing.plaf.BorderUIResource.BevelBorderUIResource).

The pattern

```
javax.swing.plaf..*
```

will match every class in javax.swing.plaf package, its subpackages, and inner classes.

Type patterns add one more wild-card character, +, which must follow a regular type name pattern and make the preceding pattern match not only its types, but also its respective subtypes.

The pattern

```
javax.swing.plaf.ComponentUI+
```

will match any descendant of the ComponentUI class, for example, ButtonUI, LabelUI, and so on.

Test Case

To illustrate the syntax and usage of different pointcuts, we need a test case. It contains two classes and one abstract aspect. Listing 11.1 shows the Pcds class.

LISTING 11.1 Pcds.java Class

```
public class Pcds                              // 10
{                                              // 11
    public int a = 5;                          // 14

    Pcds(int a)                                // 16
    {
        this.a = a;                            // 18
    }

    Pcds(String a)                             // 21
    {
        this.a = Integer.parseInt(a);          // 23
    }

    public int test(String s)                  // 26
    {
        int b=0;                               // 28
        try
        {
            b = Integer.parseInt(s);           // 31
        }
        catch(NumberFormatException e)         // 33
        {
            System.out.println("Too bad...");// 35
        }
        return a+b;                            // 37
    }
}
```

The test class Pcds.java contains one member variable, two constructors of varying signatures, and one instance method. It has more join points than you ever dreamed about, all of which will be discussed in the subsequent sections. The comments at the end of each line specify the line numbers in the file that was used for actual testing (I deleted comments generated by the version control system, so the first line in the listing in reality is line 10); changing the file will skew the results below, so be forewarned: If you change this file for your own hacking pleasure, the line numbers will not match. The same is true for the main file, shown in Listing 11.2.

LISTING 11.2 PcdMain.java Class

```
public class PcdMain                           // 10
{
    public void exec(String arg)               // 14
```

LISTING 11.2 Continued

```
    {
        Pcds p = new Pcds(6);                        // 16
        p.test(arg);                                 // 17

        Pcds q = new Pcds("6");                      // 19
        q.test(arg);                                 // 20
    }

    public static void main(String args[])           // 23
    {
        new PcdMain().exec(args[0]);                 // 25
    }
}
```

The PcdMain.java class creates an instance of itself and proceeds to create two instances of Pcds, which call their test(String) method.

The heart of the test case is the abstract aspect that is responsible for outputting the information about the join points picked by pointcuts we are going to present (see Listing 11.3.).

LISTING 11.3 PcdBase.java Aspect

```
abstract public aspect PcdBase
{
    abstract pointcut p();

    before() : p()
    && !within(PcdBase+)
    {
        System.out.println(
            thisJoinPoint.getTarget()+                         " | "+
            thisJoinPoint.getThis()+                           " | "+
            thisJoinPoint.getSignature()+                      " | "+
            thisJoinPoint.getKind()+                           " | "+
            thisJoinPoint.getSourceLocation().getFileName()+" | "+
            thisJoinPoint.getSourceLocation().getLine()+       " | "+
            "");
    }

    static
    {
```

LISTING 11.3   Continued

```
        System.out.println("Target | This | Signature | Kind | File | Line");
        System.out.println("-------|------|-----------|------|------|-----");
    }

}
```

The abstract pointcut p() is going to be our workhorse for this chapter. For each example it is going to be implemented, while the uniformity of output will be preserved by executing the same before() advice of the PcdBase aspect. Its static portion prints out the header for the output, and the advice prints out various introspection information about the current join point (details of introspection API will be discussed later in Appendix A). The before() advice is triggered by the p() pointcut and there is one more within() pointcut attached to it that prevents the aspect from advising itself and its descendants to avoid infinite recursion. The semantics of this will be explained later in this chapter.

The test case can be compiled and executed as follows:

```
>ajc PcdMain.java Pcds.java PcdBase.java PcdXXX.java
>java PcdMain 33
```

PcdXXX stands for whatever concrete aspect will be discussed at the moment, and 33 is just an integer parameter needed by the test case (any other integer will also do).

Now everything is ready for actual pointcuts. It would be helpful if you could bookmark the pages with Listing 11.1 and Listing 11.2—their line numbers will be referred to frequently.

call **Pointcut**

The primitive pointcut call picks method calls based on a static signature of the desired methods:

```
call(Signature)
```

The call pointcut can also pick calls to constructors, and any one pointcut can specify more than one method if the wild-card patterns are used in the signature. Here is an example:

```
public aspect PcdCall extends PcdBase
{
    pointcut p() : call(int Pcds.test(..));
}
```

This pointcut picks calls to all overloaded `Pcds.test()` methods (there is only one method in the test case). The `PcdCall` aspect produces the output shown in Figure 11.1.

```
Target         This           Signature            Kind          File     Ln
--------------------------------------------------------------------------------
Pcds@18dfaf    PcdMain@58610  int Pcds.test (String)   method-call   PcdMain  17
Pcds@25ab41    PcdMain@58610  int Pcds.test (String)   method-call   PcdMain  20
```

FIGURE 11.1   Output of `PcdCall` aspect.

The output will be shown, from this point forward, formatted for readability and compactness. The method `Pcds.Test()` is called twice from the same `PcdMain` object (`PcdMain@58610`) on two different target `Pcds` objects (hash numbers `10dfaf` and `25ab41`, respectively). The output also shows that the kinds of the join points are method calls, and that these calls were made on lines 17 and 20 in the file `PcdMain.java`. It is worth noting that call pointcuts refer to join points in the caller (`PcdMain` class in this example), it doesn't matter if the source code of the called method is even available—only the caller's code will be advised.

The method call pointcuts can also pick calls to constructors, which will be discussed later in the "Initialization" section.

execution **Pointcut**

The `execution` primitive pointcut represents another side of the call pointcut: It picks method or constructor execution and has a syntax similar to `call`'s:

```
execution(Signature)
```

Consider the following `PcdExecution` example:

```
public aspect PcdExecution extends PcdBase
{
    pointcut p() : execution(int Pcds.test(..));
}
```

Its output is presented in Figure 11.2.

The signature of the affected method is exactly the same on both this output and the previous output—this is the same method as specified in both pointcuts. The execution join point has the same `target` and `this` object—both are the same instance of object `Pcds` where the method was executed. And, because the method

Pcds.test() was executed twice for two different instances of the object Pcds, the instances have two distinct hash codes 18dfaf and 2498b5. The crucial difference of execution pointcut from the call is where AspectJ picks the join points. Calls are picked where they were made (lines 17 and 20 in PcdMain.java file—see the previous section's output), and executions are picked at the start of the method to be executed (line 26 in Pcds.java).

Target	This	Signature	Kind	File	Ln
Pcds@18dfaf	Pcds@18dfaf	int Pcds.test (String)	method-execution	Pcds	26
Pcds@2498b5	Pcds@2498b5	int Pcds.test (String)	method-execution	Pcds	26

FIGURE 11.2   Output of PcdExecution aspect.

The execution pointcut requires the source of the target method to be available. As we have seen, this is where the join point is picked.

get **Pointcut**

The get pointcut picks the field reference join point, the place where a value of an object field is obtained. It is based on the field signature and has the this form:

get(Signature)

Where the signature has to describe the field as declared. Consider the following aspect:

```
public aspect PcdGet extends PcdBase
{
    pointcut p() : get(int Pcds.a);
}
```

It picks all references to the Pcd.a instance variable of class Pcds and produces the output shown in Figure 11.3.

Target	This	Signature	Kind	File	Ln
Pcds@18dfaf	Pcds@18dfaf	int Pcds.a	field-get	Pcds	37
Pcds@2498b5	Pcds@2498b5	int Pcds.a	field-get	Pcds	37

FIGURE 11.3   Output of PcdGet aspect.

The figure shows that the value of this field was obtained twice at line 37 of the Pcds.java file.

set **Pointcut**

The set pointcut picks the field assignment join point and, thus, represents the mirror operation for the get pointcut with the similar syntax:

```
set(Signature)
```

This is the example:

```
public aspect PcdSet extends PcdBase
{
    pointcut p() : set(int Pcds.a);
}
```

Its output is shown in Figure 11.4.

Target	This	Signature	Kind	File	Ln
Pcds@18dfaf	Pcds@18dfaf	int Pcds.a	field-set	Pcds	14
Pcds@18dfaf	Pcds@18dfaf	int Pcds.a	field-set	Pcds	18
Pcds@2498b5	Pcds@2498b5	int Pcds.a	field-set	Pcds	14
Pcds@2498b5	Pcds@2498b5	int Pcds.a	field-set	Pcds	23

FIGURE 11.4   Output of PcdSet aspect.

The field Pcds.a is assigned in three separate places: On line 14 during initialization for each Pcds object created, and on lines 18 and 23, respectively, for Pcds's two constructors. In the example it occurs two times for each Pcds instance, and because the test program creates two of these, four join points are picked and presented in the output.

handler **Pointcut**

The handler pointcut picks an execution of an exception handler, and it accepts the type pattern of the desired Throwable object:

```
handler(TypePattern)
```

In the following PcdHandler example, the pointcut p() is asked to pick handlers for any descendant of a Throwable class, in effect, anything that can be thrown:

```
public aspect PcdHandler extends PcdBase
{
    pointcut p() : handler(Throwable+);
}
```

If you compile and execute this example as described at the beginning of this chapter, there will be no output besides the initial header. This is to be expected because no exception is thrown during the normal course of the program. The easy way to break it is to pass an unparseable integer as a parameter:

```
>java PcdMain 33XXX
```

It then produces the output shown in Figure 11.5.

Target	This	Signature	Kind	File	Ln
Pcds@18dfaf	Pcds@18dfaf	catch(NumberFormatExdception)	exception-handler	Pcds	33
Pcds@2498b5	Pcds@2498b5	catch(NumberFormatExdception)	exception-handler	Pcds	33

FIGURE 11.5   Output of `PcdHandler` aspect.

This output shows that the pointcut actually picked the exception of the type `NumberFormatException` at line 33 of the `Pcds.test()` method in the file `Pcds.java`.

Initialization

An object initialization can be captured in three possible ways: using `call`, `execution`, or `initialization` pointcuts. The first two treat constructors as regular instance methods with similar behavior.

Here is a `PcdCallConstructor` aspect:

```
public aspect PcdCallConstructor extends PcdBase
{
    pointcut p() : call(Pcds.new(..));
}
```

Its output is presented in Figure 11.6.

Target	This	Signature	Kind	File	Ln
null	PcdMain@239137	Pcds(int)	constructor-call	PcdMain	16
null	PcdMain@239137	Pcds(String)	constructor-call	PcdMain	19

FIGURE 11.6   Output of `PcdCallConstructor` aspect.

The following `PcdExecutionConstructor` aspect

```
public aspect PcdExecutionConstructor extends PcdBase
{
    pointcut p() : execution(Pcds.new(..));
}
```

produces output shown in Figure 11.7.

Target	This	Signature	Kind	File	Ln
Pcds@18dfaf	Pcds@18dfaf	Pcds(int)	constructor@execution	Pcds	16
Pcds@2498b5	Pcds@2498b5	Pcds(String)	constructor@execution	Pcds	21

FIGURE 11.7   Output of `PcdExecutionConstructor` aspect.

The only unusual thing about this pair of aspects and pointcuts is the method signature: It has no return type, and because `new()` is a Java keyword it always means constructor. The output shows that AspectJ understood it perfectly well—the kind of join points were constructor call and constructor execution, respectively. The line numbers also point to places where the constructors were explicitly invoked (lines 16 and 19 in `PcdMain.java` file) and where their respective bodies begin (lines 16 and 21 in `Pcds.java`).

At the time a constructor is called, the `target` object is set to `null` for constructor call pointcuts (see the first output) because there is no object in existence just yet. The constructor execution picks the join points inside the freshly created object, and both `target` and `this` object references point to the same currently executing object (we have created two of these—18dfaf and 2498b5 in the second output). Or, in other words, the constructor execution pointcut behaves just as the method execution would.

The `initialization` pointcut allows us to drill even deeper into the object initialization process. The syntax is

```
initialization(Signature)
```

The `Signature` is expected to be of a constructor; it will be flagged as an error otherwise. The join point it picked happens to be between the parent constructor return and the constructor matching the signature (before, after, or instead depends on what kind of advice is triggered):

```
public aspect PcdInitialization extends PcdBase
{
    pointcut p() : initialization(Pcds.new(..));
}
```

The pointcut in the `PcdInitialization` aspect picks initialization of the `Pcds` object via any of the available constructors (it has two). The output is presented in Figure 11.8.

Target	This	Signature	Kind	File	Ln
Pcds@18dfaf	Pcds@18dfaf	Pcds(int)	initialization	Pcds	11
Pcds@2498b5	Pcds@2498b5	Pcds(String)	initialization	Pcds	11

FIGURE 11.8   Output of `PcdInitialization` aspect.

Because there are two instances of Pcds object, the pointcut picked both matching constructors used to create them. The differences between outputs of this example and of the constructor execution (previous output) are in the kind of a join point (constructor execution versus initialization) and the line numbers in the Pcds.java source file. The initialization join point is indicated as being at the opening curly brace of the class Pcds (see Listing 11.1). Because it does not correspond to anything that was explicitly coded in the Pcd.java file, the opening brace is as good a place as any to indicate where the parent constructor (never mentioned in our code) would have returned.

Let's look at how ajc handled it. Here is a fragment of the compiled Pcds(int) constructor with the PcdExecutionConstructor aspect applied:

```
Pcds(int a)
{
    super();
    {
      this.a = 5;
    }
    final org.aspectj.lang.JoinPoint thisJoinPoint = ...;
    PcdExecutionConstructor.aspect$.before0$ajc(thisJoinPoint);
    this.a = a;
  }
```

And here's a fragment of Pcds.java compiled with the PcdInitialization aspect:

```
Pcds(int a)
{
    super();
    final org.aspectj.lang.JoinPoint thisJoinPoint = ...;
    PcdInitialization.aspect$.before0$ajc(thisJoinPoint);
    {
      this.a = 5;
    }
    this.a = a;
  }
```

In the case of the constructor execution pointcut, the advice PcdExecutionConstructor.aspect$.before0$ajc() runs before the constructor's body, which is represented by this statement:

```
this.a = a;
```

Naturally, this is a `before()` advice, but after the other initialization code represented by the following initial assignment construct:

```
{
   this.a = 5;
}
```

The initialization pointcut picks the join point right after the parent constructor, but before any other initialization. The advice `PcdInitialization.aspect$.before0$ajc()` runs right before the initial assignment shown previously.

If the `before()` advice in `PcdBase` abstract aspect (see Listing 11.3) is changed to become an `after()` advice, the differences in execution paths between object initialization and constructor execution virtually disappear.

Here's a fragment of `Pcds.java` compiled with the `PcdExecutionConstructor` aspect and the `after()` advice:

```
Pcds(int a)
{
    super();
    final org.aspectj.lang.JoinPoint thisJoinPoint = ...;
    try
    {
      {
         this.a = 5;
      }
      this.a = a;
    }
    finally
    {
      PcdInitialization.aspect$.after0$ajc(thisJoinPoint);
    }
  }
```

The following shows a fragment of `Pcds.java` compiled with `PcdInitialization` aspect and `after()` advice:

```
Pcds(int a)
{
    super();
    {
      this.a = 5;
    }
```

```
      final org.aspectj.lang.JoinPoint thisJoinPoint = ...;
      try
      {
        this.a = a;
      }
      finally
      {
        PcdExecutionConstructor.aspect$.after0$ajc(thisJoinPoint);
      }
  }
```

In both cases the advice runs as instructed: after object initialization and after the constructor is done.

staticinitialization **Pointcut**

The staticinitialization pointcut picks the execution of a static initializer of a class. The syntax is

```
staticinitialization(TypePattern)
```

where the TypePattern can match one or more types. The PcdStaticInitialization example follows:

```
public aspect PcdStaticInitialization extends PcdBase
{
    pointcut p() : staticinitialization(Pcds);
}
```

The pointcut picks one join point and reports it to be at the declaration line of the source file Pcds.java; output is in Figure 11.9.

Target	This	Signature	Kind	File	Ln
null	null	Pcds.<init>	staticinitialization	Pcds	10

FIGURE 11.9 Output of PcdStaticInitialization aspect.

During the static initialization, of course, there is no target or current object—the initialization is purely static. The Pcds class does not have any static initialization, but if we insert something like

```
public static int staticInt = 555;
```

then AspectJ will place the advice just before the assignment statement it generates for the `staticInt` class variable:

```
public class Pcds
{
  // ...
  public static int staticInt;
  public int a;
  //
  // ...
  //
  static
  {
    // ...
    PcdStaticInitialization.aspect$.before0$ajc(thisJoinPoint);
    Pcds.staticInt = 555;
  }
}
```

within **Pointcut**

The `within` pointcut picks join points that are found inside the classes that match the type pattern:

```
within(TypePattern)
```

But which join points are they? Unless this pointcut is combined with some other pointcuts (see the following `PcdWithin` aspect), the `within` picks all join points the AspectJ is capable of finding.

```
public aspect PcdWithin extends PcdBase
{
    pointcut p() : within(PcdMain);
}
```

For example, this `PcdWithin` aspect will pick every join point that `ajc` can detect in `PcdMain` class as shown in Figure 11.10.

Target	This	Signature	Kind	File	Ln
null	null	Pcds.<init>	staticinitialization	PcdMain	10
null	null	void Pcdmain.main(String[])	method-execution	Pcdmain	23
null	null	PcdMain()	constructor-call	PcdMain	25
Pcdmain@1fbe93	Pcdmain@1fbe93	PcdMain()	initialization	PcdMain	11
PcdMain@1fbe93	Pcdmain@1fbe93	PcdMain.<init>	instanceinitializer-execution	PcdMain	10
PcdMain@1fbe93	Pcdmain@1fbe93	PcdMain()	constructor-execution	PcdMain	10
Pcdmain@1fbe93	null	void PcdMain.exec(String)	method-call	PcdMain	25
Pcdmain@1fbe93	Pcdmain@1fbe93	void PcdMain.exec(String)	method-execution	PcdMain	14
null	Pcdmain@1fbe93	Pcds(int)	constructor-call	PcdMain	16
Pcds@41cd1f	Pcdmain@1fbe93	int Pcds.test(String)	method-call	PcdMain	17
null	Pcdmain@1fbe93	Pcds(String)	constructor-call	PcdMain	19
Pcds@1afa3	Pcdmain@1fbe93	int Pcds.test(String)	method-call	PcdMain	20

FIGURE 11.10   Output of `PcdWithin` aspect.

Usually, the `within` pointcut is qualified with some other pointcuts to localize their reach, for example, to prevent recursion or to avoid advising wrong classes.

withincode **Pointcut**

The `withincode` pointcut continues the list of the lexically oriented facilities of AspectJ. `withincode` picks join points that belong to a specific method or constructor as specified by the signature pattern:

```
withincode(Signature)
```

As in the case of `within` pointcut, the `withincode` will also pick every join point imaginable unless qualified by some other pointcuts. Consider the following PcdWithinCode example:

```
public aspect PcdWithinCode extends PcdBase
{
    pointcut p() : withincode(int Pcds.test(..));
}
```

It will pick all join points inside the `Pcds.test()` method as indicated in Figure 11.11.

Target	This	Signature	Kind	File	Ln
Pcds@18dfaf	Pcds@18dfaf	int Pcds.test(String)	method-execution	Pcds	26
null	Pcds@18dfaf	int Integer.parseInt(String)	method-call	Pcds	31
Pcds@18dfaf	Pcds@18dfaf	int Pcds.a	field-get	Pcds	37
Pcds@2498b5	Pcds@2498b5	int Pcds.test(String)	method-execution	Pcds	26
null	Pcds@2498b5	int Integer.parseInt(String)	method-call	Pcds	31
Pcds@2498b5	Pcds@2498b5	int Pcds.a	field-get	Pcds	37

FIGURE 11.11   Output of `PcdWithinCode` aspect.

There are three of these: the `test()`'s own execution, the call to `Integer.parseInt()`, and the field reference for `Pcds.a`. This sequence of join points is repeated for each call to Pcds.test(): it was called twice for objects 18dfaf and 2498b5.

Again, as with the within pointcut, the withincode is used primarily to limit the scope of other pointcuts.

cflow **Pointcut**

The cflow, and its variant cflowbelow (described in the next section), represent a very interesting concept. They are defined not in terms of type or signature patterns, but with relation to another pointcut:

```
cflow(Pointcut)
```

This means that the cflow pointcut will pick all join points encountered during the program execution starting at the join point picked by another pointcut explicitly named in the declaration. The following aspect defines pointcut p() as a cflow pointcut that uses join points of pointcut q() as a start. The latter picks calls to Pcds.test() method:

```
public aspect PcdCflow extends PcdBase
{
    pointcut p() : cflow(q());
    pointcut q() : call(int Pcds.test(..));
}
```

Figure 11.12 shows what happens when all these join points are picked.

Target	This	Signature	Kind	File	Ln
Pcds@2125f0	PcdMain@41cd1f	int Pcds.test(String)	method-call	Pcdmain	17
Pcds@2125f0	Pcds@2125f0	int Pcds.test(String)	method-execution	Pcds	26
null	Pcds@2125f0	int Integer.parseInt(String)	method-call	Pcds	31
Pcds@2125f0	Pcds@2125f0	int Pcds.a	field-get	Pcds	37
Pcds@31f71a	PcdMain@41cd1f	int Pcds.test(String)	method-call	Pcdmain	20
Pcds@31f71a	Pcds@31f71a	int Pcds.test(String)	method-execution	Pcds	26
null	Pcds@31f71a	int Integer.parseInt(String)	method-call	Pcds	31
Pcds@31f71a	Pcds@31f71a	int Pcds.a	field-get	Pcds	37

FIGURE 11.12   Output of PcdCflow aspect.

It all starts with a method call to Pcds.test() made from PcdMain class on line 17 of PcdMain.java. Note that the currently executing object is PcdMain, and the target is the first instance of Pcds (hash code 3235f0). This join point is picked by both pointcuts p() and q(). After this, p() picks the method execution of Pcds.test(), the call to Integer.parseInt(), and the field reference Pcds.a. None of this has anything to do with what q() has picked—it just picked a starting point—the original method call. The same chain of join points repeats for the second call to the

`Pcd.test()` with the same results. The first call is from the different place, but the rest presents the same path of execution, namely, the body of `Pcd.test()`, and whatever join points happened to be there are picked by the `p()` pointcut.

`cflowbelow` Pointcut

The `cflowbelow` pointcut works almost exactly as the `cflow` one, but with a notable exception: It picks only join points that are below the initial join point picked by the pointcut specified in `cflowbelow` declaration:

```
cflowbelow(Pointcut)
```

Consider the same example as in the previous section with `cflow` replaced by `cflowbelow`:

```
public aspect PcdCflowbelow extends PcdBase
{
    pointcut p() : cflowbelow(q());
    pointcut q() : call(int Pcds.test(..));
}
```

The output in Figure 11.13 is also similar.

```
Target          This            Signature                    Kind                File   Ln
--------------------------------------------------------------------------------------------
Pcds@2125f0     Pcds@2125f0     int Pcds.test(String)        method-execution    Pcds   26
null            Pcds@2125f0     int Integer.parseInt(String) method-call         Pcds   31
Pcds@2125f0     Pcds@2125f0     int Pcds.a                   field-get           Pcds   37
Pcds1afa3       Pcds1afa3       int Pcds.test(String)        method-execution    Pcds   26
null            Pcds1afa3       int Integer.parseInt(String) method-call         Pcds   31
Pcds1afa3       Pcds1afa3       int Pcds.a                   field-get           Pcds   37
```

FIGURE 11.13   Output of `PcdCflowbelow` aspect.

The notable difference is that starting calls to `Pcds.test()` are not there—only join points that follow are.

`this` Pointcut

The `this` pointcut can be used to discriminate join points based on what object is currently executing:

```
this(TypePattern|Identifier)
```

That is, it picks all join points where the type of the executing object either matches the type pattern or is of the same type as the identifier (identifiers are used for context exposure—see the section "Context" for details). Naturally, the content of all static methods is excluded—no particular object instance is associated with them. Here is the example:

```
public aspect PcdThis extends PcdBase
{
    pointcut p() : this(PcdMain);
}
```

Its output follows in Figure 11.14.

Target	This	Signature	Kind	File	Ln
PcdMain@239137	PcdMain@239137	PcdMain()	Initialization	PcdMain	11
PcdMain@239137	PcdMain@239137	PcdMain.<init>	Instanceinitializer-execution	Pcdmain	10
PcdMain@239137	PcdMain@239137	PcdMain()	constructor-execution	Pcdmain	10
PcdMain@239137	PcdMain@239137	void Pcdmain.exec(String)	method-execution	PcdMain	14
null	PcdMain@239137	Pcds(int)	constructor-call	PcdMain	16
Pcds@2498b5	PcdMain@239137	int Pcds.test(String)	method-call	PcdMain	17
null	PcdMain@239137	Pcds(String)	constructor-call	PcdMain	19
Pcds@25ab41	PcdMain@239137	int Pcds.test(String)	method-call	PcdMain	20

FIGURE 11.14   Output of PcdThis aspect.

All join points associated with the one and only instance of PcdMain are shown: initialization, constructor execution, execution of the PcdMain.exec() method, calls to Pcds's constructors, and the Pcd.test() method—nothing else happened with it.

target Pointcut

The target pointcut in some ways is similar to the this pointcut because it picks join points according to the object type. In this case, however, it is a target object of the join point:

```
target(TypePattern|Identifier)
```

The target means an instance of an object to which the picked operation is applied. Exclusion of the static content equally applies here, too.

The following PcdTarget aspect will detect all join points where instances of Pcds class were targeted:

```
public aspect PcdTarget extends PcdBase
{
    pointcut p() : target(Pcds);
}
```

And it produces what is presented in Figure 11.15.

Target	This	Signature	Kind	File	Ln
Pcds@18dfaf	Pcds@18dfaf	Pcds(int)	initialization	Pcds	11
Pcds@18dfaf	Pcds@18dfaf	Pcds.<init>	instanceinitializer-execution	Pcds	10
Pcds@18dfaf	Pcds@18dfaf	int Pcds.a	field-set	Pcds	14
Pcds@18dfaf	Pcds@18dfaf	Pcds(int)	constructor-execution	Pcds	16
Pcds@18dfaf	Pcds@18dfaf	int Pcds.a	field-set	Pcds	18
Pcds@18dfaf	Pcds@18dfaf	int Pcds.test(String)	method-call	PcdMain	17
Pcds@18dfaf	Pcds@18dfaf	int Pcds.test(String)	method-execution	Pcds	26
Pcds@18dfaf	Pcds@18dfaf	int Pcds.a	field-get	Pcds	37
Pcds@41cd1f	Pcds@41cd1f	Pcds(String)	initialization	Pcds	11
Pcds@41cd1f	Pcds@41cd1f	Pcds.<init>	instanceinitializer-execution	Pcds	10
Pcds@41cd1f	Pcds@41cd1f	int Pcds.a	field-set	Pcds	14
Pcds@41cd1f	Pcds@41cd1f	Pcds(String)	constructor-execution	Pcds	21
Pcds@41cd1f	Pcds@41cd1f	int Pcds.a	field-set	Pcds	23
Pcds@41cd1f	PcdMain@2498b5	int Pcds.test(String)	method-call	PcdMain	20
Pcds@41cd1f	Pcds@41cd1f	int Pcds.test(String)	method-execution	Pcds	26
Pcds@41cd1f	Pcds@41cd1f	int Pcds.a	field-get	Pcds	37

FIGURE 11.15   Output of `PcdTarget` aspect.

The output shows exactly what was happening with the two instances of the `Pcds` class starting with construction and ending with the field access; it follows the execution path of the program.

args **Pointcut**

The args pointcut is used almost exclusively for context exposure (we have to postpone this discussion again until the upcoming "Context" section), but it can produce very interesting results on its own right:

```
args(TypePattern|Identifier, ...)
```

It picks join points whose arguments are instances of types matching the type pattern or the type of the identifier. Several type patterns or identifiers might be present separated by commas, as in a method signature.

The pointcut p() of the following aspect will pick all join points that has an argument of type int:

```
public aspect PcdArgs extends PcdBase
{
    pointcut p() : args(int);
}
```

And there are plenty of these, as evident from Figure 11.16.

One of the `Pcds` constructors takes an integer argument, so calls to it, its initialization, and execution are all picked by the pointcut. Setting an integer field also takes an implicit integer argument, so all assignments to `Pcds.a` instance variable are also present.

```
Target          This            Signature       Kind                    File      Ln
--------------------------------------------------------------------------------------
null            PcdMain@239137  Pcds(int)       constructor-call        PcdMain   16
Pcds@2498b5     Pcds@2498b5     Pcds(int)       initialization          Pcds      11
Pcds@2498b5     Pcds@2498b5     int Pcds.a      field-set               Pcds      14
Pcds@2498b5     Pcds@2498b5     Pcds(int)       constructor-execution   Pcds      16
Pcds@2498b5     Pcds@2498b5     int Pcds.a      field-set               Pcds      18
Pcds@25ab41     Pcds@25ab41     int Pcds.a      field-set               Pcds      14
Pcds@25ab41     Pcds@25ab41     int Pcds.a      field-set               Pcds      23
```

FIGURE 11.16   Output of `PcdArgs` aspect.

if **Pointcut**

The `if` primitive pointcut picks all joint points based on the result of the Boolean expression specified in its declaration:

```
if(BooleanExpr)
```

BooleanExpr should be a valid Java logical expression. For example:

```
public aspect PcdIf extends PcdBase
{
    pointcut p() :
    if( thisJoinPoint.getTarget() == null
        && thisJoinPoint.getThis() == null);
}
```

This aspect's pointcut must find all join points, which have `targets` and `these` (pun intended) equal to `null`. They are displayed in Figure 11.17.

```
Target      This      ignature                    Kind                    File      Ln
--------------------------------------------------------------------------------------
null        null      PcdMain.<init>              staticinitialization    PcdMain   10
null        null      void PcdMain.main(String[]) method-execution        PcdMain   23
null        null      PcdMain()                   constructor-call        PcdMain   25
null        null      Pcds.<init>                 staticinitialization    PcdMain   10
```

FIGURE 11.17   Output of `PcdIf` aspect.

Note that the Boolean expression will be evaluated at runtime and must be valid in then current context.

PointcutId **Pointcut**

You can express pointcuts in terms of some other pointcuts, and `PointcutId` is specifically designed for this purpose:

```
PointcutId(TypePattern|Identifier, ...)
```

It picks exactly the same join points as the original pointcut. This language construct is needed for combining primitive pointcuts into rather complex ones and for passing their parameters around. The discussion about the context exposure is slowly, but surely, creeping in.

By itself the `PointcutId` is not that exciting. The necessity of it will become apparent in the next several sections where combining pointcuts will be described. In formulating new pointcuts you can use not only primitive pointcuts, but also previously defined pointcuts referred to by their respective names, thus, implicitly invoking the `PointcutId` syntax. Here is the simplest case:

```
public aspect PcdId extends PcdBase
{
    pointcut a(String x) : args(x);
    pointcut p() : a(String);
}
```

The pointcut `p()` is declared using the `a()` pointcut that happens to have a parameter of type `String`. This declaration is equivalent to the one in the section "args Pointcut." The only difference is that `p()` will pick `a()`'s type—all join points where argument is a `String`. The results are in Figure 11.18.

Target	This	Signature	Kind	File	Ln
PcdMain@239137	null	void PcdMain.exec(String)	method-call	PcdMain	25
PcdMain@239137	PcdMain@239137	void PcdMain.exec(String)	method-execution	PcdMain	14
Pcds@2498b5	PcdMain@239137	int Pcds.test(String)	method-call	PcdMain	17
Pcds@2498b5	Pcds@2498b5	int Pcds.test(String)	method-execution	PcdMain	26
null	Pcds@2498b5	int parseInt(String)	method-call	PcdMain	31
null	PcdMain@239137	Pcds(String)	constructor-call	PcdMain	19
Pcds@25ab41	Pcds@25ab41	Pcds(String)	Initialization	Pcds	11
Pcds@25ab41	Pcds@25ab41	Pcds(String)	constructor-execution	Pcds	21
null	Pcds@25ab41	int Integer.parseInt(String)	method-call	PcdMain	23
Pcds@25ab41	PcdMain@239137	int Pcds.test(String)	method-call	PcdMain	20
Pcds@25ab41	Pcds@25ab41	int Pcds.test(String)	method-execution	PcdMain	26
null	Pcds@25ab41	int Integer.parseInt(String)	method-call	PcdMain	31

FIGURE 11.18 Output of `PcdId` aspect.

All picked join points are related to three entities that take `String` as an argument: a constructor `Pcd(String)`, static method `Integer.parseInt(String)`, and the instance method `Pcds.text(String)`.

The ! Operation

This pointcut

```
!Pointcut
```

will pick all join points not picked by the declared pointcut. Consider the following PcdNot example:

```
public aspect PcdNot extends PcdBase
{
    pointcut p() : !args(*);
}
```

args(*) picks join points with exactly one argument of any type. If these join points were excluded from the list of all detectable join points, the remaining join points will have to take either more than one argument or none at all. Our test case does not have the former, so the negating args(*) pointcut will produce the list of join points that do not have any arguments as shown in Figure 11.19.

```
Target            This              Signature         Kind                               File    Ln
-----------------------------------------------------------------------------------------------------------
null              null              PcdMain.<init>    staticinitialization               Pcdmain 10
null              null              PcdMain()         constructor-call                   PcdMain 25
PcdMain@12e78c    PcdMain@12e78c    PcdMain()         initialization                     PcdMain 11
PcdMain@12e78c    PcdMain@12e78c    PcdMain.<init>    instanceinitializer-execution      PcdMain 10
PcdMain@12e78c    PcdMain@12e78c    PcdMain()         constructor-execution              PcdMain 10
null              null              Pcds.<init>       staticinitialization               Pcds    10
Pcds@2498b5       Pcds@2498b5       Pcds.<init>       instanceinitializer-execution      Pcds    10
Pcds@2498b5       Pcds@2498b5       int Pcds.a        field-get                          Pcds    37
Pcds@41cd1f       Pcds@41cd1f       Pcds.<init>       instanceinitializer-execution      Pcds    10
Pcds@41cd1f       Pcds@41cd1f       int Pcds.a        field-get                          Pcds    37
```

FIGURE 11.19   Output of PcdNot aspect.

NOTE

Please note that in this section, and the several subsequent ones, the pointcuts are combined in what looks like Boolean expressions using !, ||, and &&. The appearance of them as such is almost coincidental. In reality, they are all operations on join point sets, meaning that the result of a pointcut is not a Boolean value (true or false), but rather a set of join points that the pointcut picks. Therefore, the expression !pointcut does not mean "not the pointcut," but instead means "from the set of all available join points throw away the ones picked by the pointcut."

The && Operation

The join points picked by two pointcuts might be combined by the && operation:

```
Pointcut1 && Pointcut2
```

This would mean that the resulting set of join points must contain only the join points picked by both pointcuts. That is, the result is the intersection of these two sets of join points. Consider the following example:

```
public aspect PcdAnd extends PcdBase
{
    pointcut p() : this(PcdMain) && target(Pcds);
}
```

That is, the selected join points must have their execution object of type `PcdMain` and their target of type `Pcds`. This rare combination happens only when calls are made from `PcdMain` on `Pcds` methods as presented in Figure 11.20.

Target	This	Signature	Kind	File	Ln
Pcds@18dfaf	PcdMain@58610	int Pcds.test (String)	method-call	PcdMain	17
Pcds@25ab41	PcdMain@58610	int Pcds.test (String)	method-call	PcdMain	20

FIGURE 11.20 Output of `PcdAnd` aspect.

The || Operation

The || operation combines the join points picked by two pointcuts:

```
Pointcut1 || Pointcut2
```

In other words, the resulting set of join points will contain the ones present in either one of the subsets picked by their respective pointcuts. The following aspect is expected to produce the list of join points that represent calls to the `Pcds(int)` constructor, or calls to any method of any class that has one single parameter of type `String`:

```
public aspect PcdOr extends PcdBase
{
    pointcut p() : call(Pcds.new(int)) || call(* *(String));
}
```

Figure 11.21 proves that it indeed does.

Target	This	Signature	Kind	File	Ln
PcdMain@239137	null	void Pcdmain.exec(String)	method-call	Pcdmain	25
null	PcdMain@239137	Pcds(int)	constructor-call	PcdMain	16
Pcds@2498b5	PcdMain@239137	int Pcds.test(String)	method-call	Pcdmain	17
null	Pcds@2498b5	int Integer.parseInt(String)	method-call	Pcds	31
null	Pcds@25ab41	int Integer.parseInt(String)	method-call	Pcds	23
Pcds@25ab41	PcdMain@239137	int Pcds.test(String)	method-call	Pcdmain	20
null	Pcds@25ab41	int Integer.parseInt(String)	method-call	Pcds	31

FIGURE 11.21 Output of `PcdOr` aspect.

Using Parentheses

Parenthesizing pointcuts enables you to obtain complex sets of join points by combining the results of primitive pointcuts into arbitrary expressions. The parentheses pick exactly the same join points as picked by enclosed pointcuts:

```
(Pointcut)
```

By grouping the pointcuts into set expressions, the results can be rather precise:

```
public aspect PcdParenthesis extends PcdBase
{
    pointcut p() :
         !(this(PcdMain) && target(Pcds))
         &&
         !(args(int) || args(String));
}
```

The `PcdParenthesis` aspect will print join points where the single argument is neither type `int` nor type `String`. And, among them, it will only print join points whose target is not of type `Pcds` while executing inside `PcdMain` as shown in Figure 11.22.

Target	This	Signature	Kind	File	Ln
null	null	PcdMain.<init>	staticinitialization	PcdMain	10
null	null	void PcdMain.main(String[])	method-execution	PcdMain	23
null	null	PcdMain()	constructor-call	PcdMain	25
PcdMain@1fbe93	PcdMain@1fbe93	PcdMain()	initialization	PcdMain	11
PcdMain@1fbe93	PcdMain@1fbe93	PcdMain.<init>	instanceinitializer-execution	PcdMain	10
PcdMain@1fbe93	PcdMain@1fbe93	PcdMain()	constructor-execution	PcdMain	10
null	null	Pcds.<init>	staticinitialization	Pcds	10
Pcds@25ab41	Pcds@25ab41	Pcds.<init>	instanceinitializer-execution	Pcds	10
Pcds@25ab41	Pcds@25ab41	int Pcds.a	field-get	Pcds	37
Pcds@1afa3	Pcds@1afa3	Pcds.<init>	instanceinitializer-execution	Pcds	10
Pcds@1afa3	Pcds@1afa3	int Pcds.a	field-get	Pcds	37

FIGURE 11.22   Output of `PcdParenthesis` aspect.

Context

Pointcuts would only be half as useful if not for the context exposure feature: Pointcuts do allow passing parameters to their advices if the parameters are properly exposed. The syntax is very similar to Java's usual formal parameters: Typed parameters are specified in the declaration of pointcuts and advices. In the body of the pointcut, declaration parameters' names can be used in place of their respective types by three special primitive pointcuts—this, target, and args—and this is the only way the parameters can be exposed. The exposed parameters can be treated inside of advices just as Java's formal method parameters.

Consider the following example of a `ParamMain` class:

```
public class ParamMain
{
    public void exec(int a, String b)
    {
    }

    public static void main(String args[])
    {
        new ParamMain().exec(3, "5.5");
    }
}
```

The `main()` method of this class just creates an instance of itself and calls the `exec()` method. The method takes two parameters of type `int` and `String`, respectively. The `ParamMain` class is advised by the following aspect:

```
public aspect ParamAspect
{
    pointcut q(ParamMain obj) :
        execution(* *.exec(int, String)) && target(obj);
    before(ParamMain obj) : q(obj)
    {
        System.out.println("q(): "+obj.getClass().getName());
    }

    pointcut r(int x, String y) :
        call(* *.exec(int, String)) && args(x, y);
    before(int x, String y) : r(x, y)
    {
        System.out.println("r(): "+x+" and "+y);
    }
}
```

Pointcut `q()` declares one formal parameter `obj` of the type `ParamMain`. It is exposed by the primitive pointcut `target`, and as such, it can be used inside the `before()` advice triggered by the pointcut `q()`. Overall, the pointcut declaration means the following: Pick the join points when a method of any class called `exec()` that accepts two parameters is executed and the target is of type `ParamMain`.

Pointcut `r()` is similarly constructed, but exposes actual arguments passed to the method `exec()` when called. Here is the output:

```
r(): 3 and 5.5
q(): ParamMain
```

The value of the formal parameters can be freely used; in our example, they are just printed out.

The exposed formal parameters can also be obtained by using the introspection API calls getThis(), getTarget(), and getArgs() instead of this, target, and args pointcuts, respectively. The difference is that pointcuts parameters provide compile time-type safety and are guaranteed to be there at runtime by virtue of implied pointcut operations. For example, the target(TypeX) pointcut picks only TypeX targets and is guaranteed to be not null. If JoinPoint.getTarget() method is used inside the advice, nothing can be said about the target's type or even its presence at whatever join point would be currently executing.

Summary

In this chapter you've seen what a powerful pointcut language exists for finding join points. Combining various pointcuts and exposing their execution context allows you to pinpoint exact places in a program's structure and access (and modify if necessary) its runtime environment—and all this functionality is available in a reliable, type-safe manner.

12

Advices

In this chapter we will examine the executable portion of aspects—the *advice*. An advice's behavior is closely related to the behavior of Java's methods, but there are some additional rules that we will have to discuss.

Introductory Notes

An advice defines what code should run at join points that are picked out by pointcuts; in other words, it actually contains the implementation of the crosscutting logic. An advice can be triggered by named or nameless pointcuts and can have formal parameters that are either provided by the pointcuts or exposed by the advice itself. The code in the advice can throw exceptions, but you have to be careful about it because the exceptions have to match the join point context unless they are `RuntimeExceptions`. In other words, if a join point, for example, is a call to a method that does not declare any exceptions, throwing an exception from the advice will be flagged as a compilation error because target code (where the join point is) would not know how to handle it. Another matter of concern is handling join points that cannot possibly throw any exception, for example, field gets. Table 12.1 will help to navigate.

TABLE 12.1 Exception Compatibility Chart

Join point	Allowable exceptions (non-runtime)
Method call or execution	Declared by the method
Constructor call or execution	Declared by the constructor
Field get and set	None
Exception handler	Handled on upper level, that is, by the enclosing try-catch block or declared by the target's method

TABLE 12.1   Continued

Join point	Allowable exceptions (non-runtime)
Static initializer	None
Initializer execution, preinitialization, initialization	Declared by all constructors of the class to be initialized

The three basic kinds of advices are before, after, and around. The after advice has variations based on some runtime properties of the advised join point (see the section "The after Advice"). Advices can have return statements inside of them, but they have to return nothing for before() and after() advices. A return statement inside an around() advice has to return the declared type (see Listing 12.1).

To illustrate the behavior of all kinds of advices, we will need the test class in Listing 12.1.

LISTING 12.1   AdviceMain.java Class

```java
public class AdviceMain
{
    static public String className(Object o)
    {
        String name = "none";
        if(null != o)
        {
            name = o.getClass().getName();
        }
        return name;
    }

    public int intStr(String s) throws Exception
    {
        System.out.println("Inside intStr() method.");

        int b;
        try
        {
            b = Integer.parseInt(s);
        }
        catch(NumberFormatException e)
        {
```

LISTING 12.1   Continued

```
            throw new Exception("Bad format.");
        }
        return b;
    }

    public String strStr(String s)
    {
        System.out.println("Inside strStr() method.");

        int b = Integer.parseInt(s);
        return Integer.toString(b);
    }

    public void voidStr(String s) throws IllegalAccessException
    {
        System.out.println("Inside voidStr() method.");

        int b;
        try
        {
            b = Integer.parseInt(s);
        }
        catch(NumberFormatException e)
        {
            throw new IllegalAccessException("Bad format.");
        }

        return;
    }

    public static void main(String args[])
    {
        AdviceMain am = new AdviceMain();
        try
        {
            am.intStr(args[0]);
        }
        catch(Throwable e)
        {
            System.out.println("Got :"+e);
        }
```

LISTING 12.1   Continued

```
        try
        {
            am.strStr(args[0]);
        }
        catch(Throwable e)
        {
            System.out.println("Got :"+e);
        }

        try
        {
            am.voidStr(args[0]);
        }
        catch(Throwable e)
        {
            System.out.println("Got :"+e);
        }
    }
}
```

This class has three instance methods, strStr(), intStr(), and voidStr(), that accept one String argument and return values of different types: String, int, and void, respectively. Each of the methods tries to parse its String argument as int and throws various exceptions if it is not possible. The intStr() method throws Exception, the strStr() method does not do anything special, so NumberFormatException (a RuntimeException) is automatically rethrown, and voidStr() throws IllegalAccessException (do not read too much into this; it's just an example of a non-RuntimeException).

The main() method creates an instance of the class and calls all three of these methods; carefully wrapping each call into a try-catch block to examine exceptions, if any. The utility method, className(), is just a null-safe wrapper written to obtain an object's class name—we will need it in the advices.

To compile and execute the examples in this chapter the following commands can be used:

```
>ajc AdviceMain.java AdviceXXX.java
>java AdviceMain 33
```

In these commands, *AdviceXXX* stands for whatever concrete aspect will be compiled with the AdviceMain class, and 33 is a command-line argument.

Now we are ready to proceed.

The before Advice

The before advice has the form

```
before(FormalParameters) : Pointcut {Body}
```

The advice's body is executed before the join point picked by its pointcut is reached. Let's consider the following AdviceBefore.java aspect:

```
public aspect AdviceBefore
{
    before() : call(* AdviceMain.*Str(..))
    {
        System.out.println(thisJoinPoint);
    }
}
```

Its only advice is triggered by a nameless pointcut that picks calls for methods of the AdviceMain class whose names end with Str, for example, strStr(), intStr(), and voidStr() (the same pointcut will be used in the following sections, so we can compare the results). While executed, it produces the following unremarkable output (slightly formatted for presentation):

```
call(int AdviceMain.intStr(String))
Inside intStr() method.
call(String AdviceMain.strStr(String))
Inside strStr() method.
call(void AdviceMain.voidStr(String))
Inside voidStr() method.
```

The output shows, as expected, that there were three calls to these methods and that nothing else special happened. The before advice is the most straightforward advice among them all.

The after Advice

The goal of the after advice is to execute its body after the corresponding join point. The problem is that not all cases of after are created equal. What if an exception is thrown while at the join point? To address this issue, AspectJ provides the three versions of the `after` advice: a simple form that runs the body regardless of circumstances, a form that runs only after normal return from the join point, and the one that only reacts on exceptions.

The simplest form—the one that always runs—is similar in syntax to the `before` advice:

```
after(FormalParameters) : Pointcut {Body}
```

The following `AdviceAfter.java` example also executes similarly to the `AdviceBefore` aspect, but only after the calls return:

```
public aspect AdviceAfter
{
    after() : call(* AdviceMain.*Str(..))
    {
        System.out.println(thisJoinPoint);
    }
}
```

Here is the output for that aspect. Inside intStr() method.

```
Here is the output for that aspect.Inside intStr()  method.
call(int    AdviceMain.intStr( String))
Inside strStr()  method.
call(String AdviceMain.strStr( String))
Inside voidStr()  method.
call(void   AdviceMain.voidStr(String))
```

Comparing the previous ouput listing with this one makes the differences immediately apparent. The output from inside the `AdviceMain`'s methods precedes the output from the aspect's methods.

If the advised method throws an exception (we can provoke that by passing an unparsable integer as a parameter, for example, 33a instead of the usual 33), the output changes, but the behavior of advices do not:

```
Inside intStr() method.
call(int    AdviceMain.intStr( String))
Got :java.lang.Exception: Bad format.
Inside strStr()  method.
call(String AdviceMain.strStr( String))
Got :java.lang.NumberFormatException: 33a
Inside voidStr()  method.
call(void    AdviceMain.voidStr(String))
Got :java.lang.IllegalAccessException: Bad format.
```

This means that the advices keep executing, even after an exception was thrown—note that they execute before the exceptions were handled inside `AdviceMain.main()` method.

The after returning Advice

The `returning` version of the `after` advice runs only if the code at the join points executes normally, without throwing any exceptions. The syntax is as follows:

```
after(FormalParameters) returning [(OneFormalParameter)]: Pointcut {Body}
```

In addition to the parameters provided by the pointcut, the advice can have one more. It can have the object returned at the join point if that object is exposed by providing its definition directly after the `returning` keyword. Consider the following `AdviceAfterReturning.java` example:

```java
public aspect AdviceAfterReturning
{
    // 1
    after() returning(Object o) : call(* AdviceMain.*Str(..))
    {
        System.out.println("#1: "+thisJoinPoint+" Returning Object: "+
                        AdviceMain.className(o)+" - "+o);
    }


    // 2
    after() returning(int o) : call(* AdviceMain.*Str(..))
    {
        System.out.println("#2: "+thisJoinPoint+" Returning int: "+
                        "int"+" - "+o);
    }


    // 3
    after() returning(String o) : call(* AdviceMain.*Str(..))
    {
        System.out.println("#3: "+thisJoinPoint+" Returning String: "+
                        AdviceMain.className(o)+" - "+o);
    }


    // 4
    after() returning : call(* AdviceMain.*Str(..))
    {
        System.out.println("#4: "+thisJoinPoint+" Returning anything.");
    }
}
```

Because advices by definition cannot have names, they are just numbered in the comment lines that precede them. Advices 1 through 3 expose the returned object and declared to run if (and only if) the join point (in this case the method call) returns the specified types: `Object`, primitive type `int`, and `String`, respectively. Advice #4 should run if the advised code returns at all—that is, it is not terminated by throwing an exception. Here is the output of the test run:

```
Inside intStr() method.
#1: call(int     AdviceMain.intStr( String)) Returning Object: java.lang.Integer -
33
#2: call(int     AdviceMain.intStr( String)) Returning int: int - 33
#4: call(int     AdviceMain.intStr( String)) Returning anything.
Inside strStr() method.
#1: call(String AdviceMain.strStr( String)) Returning Object: java.lang.String - 33
#3: call(String AdviceMain.strStr( String)) Returning String: java.lang.String - 33
#4: call(String AdviceMain.strStr( String)) Returning anything.
Inside voidStr() method.
#1: call(void    AdviceMain.voidStr(String)) Returning Object: none - null
#3: call(void    AdviceMain.voidStr(String)) Returning String: none - null
#4: call(void    AdviceMain.voidStr(String)) Returning anything.
```

Wow! Looks like the `after returning` advice is a universe of its own. Let's take a closer look.

After the first method call (the one that returns primitive type `int`), advices #1, #2, and #4 run. Advice #1 thinks that the returned value of the method is `java.lang.Integer` and that being a descendant of `Object` qualifies it to be included. This gives us an insight into how AspectJ handles this: All primitive types are wrapped in its corresponding wrapper types until the intrinsic value is needed, and then it is unwrapped, as in advice #2. Advice #2 runs without any surprises treating the primitive `int` as it should be—primitive. Finally, advice #4 runs because there were no exceptions, but no return object is available because it was not exposed.

After the second method call (to the method returning `String`) a different set of advices run: #1, #3, and #4. #1 runs because `String` is an `Object`, and #4 ran because it always does. Advice #3 correctly matched the `String` return type, and #2 that should not have matched, obviously did not.

The call to the method that does not return anything, (`void AdviceMain.voidStr()`), is curious indeed. First of all, advice #1 did run, indicating that internally the AspectJ void is treated as a `null` object. Second, advice #4 legitimately ran as always. The presence of #3 cannot be explained, but a bug in the compiler is suspected because void cannot be dressed as `String` no matter what. (Please, alert me if you know of a better explanation.)

In the case of methods throwing exceptions, none of the advices should run:

```
Inside intStr() method.
Got :java.lang.Exception: Bad format.
Inside strStr() method.
Got :java.lang.NumberFormatException: 33a
Inside voidStr() method.
Got :java.lang.IllegalAccessException: Bad format.
```

The after throwing Advice

The after throwing advices run precisely when after returning do not—when an exception is thrown at the join point. The syntax enables you to expose the thrown exception that becomes available in the advice's body along with other formal parameters:

```
after(FormalParameters) throwing [(OneFormalParameter)]: Pointcut {Body}
```

The following AdviceAfterThrowing.java example tries to exhaust all possibilities (all advices are numbered as described in the previous section):

```
public aspect AdviceAfterThrowing
{
    // 1
    after() throwing(Exception o) : call(* AdviceMain.*Str(..))
    {
        System.out.println("#1: "+thisJoinPoint+" Throwing Exception: "+
                        AdviceMain.className(o)+" - "+o);
    }

    // 2
    after() throwing(RuntimeException o) : call(* AdviceMain.*Str(..))
    {
        System.out.println("#2: "+thisJoinPoint+" Throwing RuntimeException: "+
                        AdviceMain.className(o)+" - "+o);
    }

    // 3
    after() throwing : call(* AdviceMain.*Str(..))
    {
        System.out.println("#3: "+thisJoinPoint+" Throwing anything.");
    }
}
```

The first advice runs if an Exception is thrown; the second, if it was RuntimeException; and the third, if any exception whatsoever occurs. The exception objects are exposed the same way as the results in advice returning case.

During the normal course of execution nothing happens:

```
Inside intStr() method.
Inside strStr() method.
Inside voidStr() method.
```

Things get interesting when methods start throwing exceptions (I've added line breaks so the output would fit the page):

```
Inside intStr() method.
#1: call(int AdviceMain.intStr(String)) Throwing Exception:
                                Exception - java.lang.Exception: Bad format.
#3: call(int AdviceMain.intStr(String)) Throwing anything.
Got :java.lang.Exception: Bad format.

Inside strStr() method.
#1: call(String AdviceMain.strStr(String)) Throwing Exception:
      java.lang.NumberFormatException - java.lang.NumberFormatException: 33a
#2: call(String AdviceMain.strStr(String)) Throwing RuntimeException:
          java.lang.NumberFormatException - java.lang.NumberFormatException: 33a
#3: call(String AdviceMain.strStr(String)) Throwing anything.
Got :java.lang.NumberFormatException: 33a

Inside voidStr() method.
#1: call(void AdviceMain.voidStr(String)) Throwing Exception:
   java.lang.IllegalAccessException - java.lang.IllegalAccessException: Bad format.
#3: call(void AdviceMain.voidStr(String)) Throwing anything.
Got :java.lang.IllegalAccessException: Bad format.
```

Advice #1 always runs and every exception thrown is either an Exception itself or its subclass. The exposed exception object for all three method calls exhibits its true type: Exception, NumberFormatException, and IllegalAccessException for intStr(), strStr(), and voidStr(), respectively.

Advice #3 runs every time an exception is thrown, no matter what type.

The only time advice #2 runs is when the NumberFormatException is thrown from the strStr() method. It is a subtype of the RuntimeException and, therefore, matches the exception type of advice #2. The IllegalAccessException thrown from the voidStr() method is advised only by advice #1—there is no advice explicitly declared to handle this particular exception type.

Also, please note that the exception objects in after throwing and the return objects in after returning advices are matched based on their types, not on their name patterns as was the case with pointcuts. The difference can be summarized this way: The advice's decision about when to run is based on what the object really is, not on what it looks like. The word "is" is meant strictly in terms of Java's instanceof operator. For example, in the case of this advice:

```
after throwing (Throwable e) : …
```

throwing any exception whatsoever will run it. Similarly, the following advice:

```
after returning (Object o) : …
```

will always run if the join point does not end with an exception.

The around Advice

The around advice is one of the most powerful features of the AspectJ language. It enables you to replace the join point with an arbitrary code, thus making this type of advice very invasive. The syntax of it is reminiscent of regular Java methods:

```
ReturnType around(FormalParameters) [throws ListOfExceptionTypes] :
                                            Pointcut {Body}
```

The rules regarding the exceptions discussed at the beginning of this chapter still apply. Therefore, the around advice should not throw anything that the targeted code cannot handle. Inside of the advice's body a special call syntax, which follows, is provided to run the code at the original join point.

```
proceed(arguments);
```

The proceed() takes the arguments exposed by the advice's pointcut and should return the advice's declared type. If no parameters are exposed, proceed() does not need any arguments, as in the following AdviceAround.java example:

```
public aspect AdviceAround
{
    Object around() : call(* AdviceMain.*Str(..))
    {
        Object result = proceed();

        System.out.println(thisJoinPoint+" Result: "+
                            AdviceMain.className(result)+" - "+result);
        return result;
    }
}
```

The aspect prints the join point identifying information along with the result of the proceed() pseudo-call. Here is the output:

```
Inside intStr() method.
call(int    AdviceMain.intStr( String)) Result: java.lang.Integer · 33
Inside strStr() method.
call(String AdviceMain.strStr( String)) Result: java.lang.String  · 33
Inside voidStr() method.
call(void   AdviceMain.voidStr(String)) Result: none          · null
```

The result of the intStr() call—primitive int—is wrapped in java.lang.Integer, whereas the result of the method returning nothing—voidStr()—is represented as null, meaning, primitive types will be converted as needed.

The previous example can be modified to expose the argument of the method calls at the join points:

```
public aspect AdviceAroundParams
{
    Object around(String s) : call(* AdviceMain.*Str(String)) && args(s)
    {
        Object result = proceed(s);

        System.out.println(thisJoinPoint+" Parameter: ["+s+
            "] Result: "+AdviceMain.className(result)+" · "+result);
        return result;
    }
}
```

The String parameter is declared for the around() advice and it has to be exposed by the pointcut and passed to the proceed() pseudo-call. The parameter is printed out for demonstration:

```
Inside intStr() method.
call(int AdviceMain.intStr(String)) Parameter: [33]
                                        Result: java.lang.Integer · 33
Inside strStr() method.
call(String AdviceMain.strStr(String)) Parameter: [33]
                                        Result: java.lang.String · 33
Inside voidStr() method.
call(void AdviceMain.voidStr(String)) Parameter: [33]
                                        Result: none · null
```

Precedence Rules

Because an aspect can contain as many advices as needed, the issue of precedence arises for advices that are triggered on the same join point. For advices belonging to different aspects it resolves easily: The advices' precedence follows the precedence of their respective aspects, as described in Chapter 10, "Aspects," in the section titled "Domination."

For advices declared within one aspect, their precedence is determined by applying two rules:

- The precedence follows the order in which advices are declared. Meaning, if one advice is declared earlier in the text of an aspect than another, the former has higher precedence.

- Two after advices are applied in the reverse order of their declaration. Contrary to the first rule, the after advice declared earlier has lower precedence than another after advice declared later.

Consider the example in Listing 12.2.

LISTING 12.2   AdvicePrecedence.java Aspect

```
public aspect AdvicePrecedence
{
    pointcut p(): call(* AdviceMain.intStr(..));

    // after 1
    after() : p()
    {
        System.out.println("After  1");
    }

    // after 2
    after() returning(int o) : p()
    {
        System.out.println("After  2");
    }

    // before 1
    before() : p()
    {
        System.out.println("Before 1");
    }
```

LISTING 12.2   Continued

```
// before 2
before() : p()
{
    System.out.println("Before 2");
}

// around 1
int around() : p()
{
    System.out.println("Around 1 - before proceed");
    int result = proceed();
    System.out.println("Around 1 - after  proceed");
    return result;
}

// around 2
int around() : p()
{
    System.out.println("Around 2 - before proceed");
    int result = proceed();
    System.out.println("Around 2 - after  proceed");
    return 5;
}
}
```

The aspect declares one pointcut—a call to `intStr()` method of `AdviceMain` class—
and six advices; two of each major kind. Here is the output:

```
Before 1
Before 2
Around 1 - before proceed
Around 2 - before proceed
Inside intStr() method.
After  2
After  1
Around 2 - after  proceed
Around 1 - after  proceed
Inside strStr() method.
Inside voidStr() method.
```

The advices run in the order they were declared with the exception of the after advices for which the order was reversed.

Let's change the last around advice so it doesn't call proceed():

```
// around 2
int around() : p()
{
    System.out.println("Around 2 - no proceed");
    return 5;
}
```

The output will change to

```
Before 1
Before 2
Around 1 - before proceed
Around 2 - no proceed
Around 1 - after  proceed
Inside strStr() method.
Inside voidStr() method.
```

This means than the after advices have never run because, from their standpoint, the call to AspectMain.intStr() has never happened—it was replaced by the body of the second around advice. Similarly, the execution of advices' code can be severely constrained if the expected workflow is changed by other advices or exceptions. For example, if the second before advice throws an exception, as listed here:

```
// before 2
before() throws Exception : p()
{
    throw new Exception("Before 2 exception.");
}
```

the execution order will change to the following:

```
Before 1
Got :java.lang.Exception: Before 2 exception.
Inside strStr() method.
Inside voidStr() method.
```

In other words, no other advice was able to run after the second before advice has thrown an exception.

Summary

In this chapter, we discussed how the crosscutting logic is implemented. AspectJ provides rather sophisticated language facilities to develop advices that will execute exactly when needed. You need to exercise some caution with regard to exceptions and formal advice parameters. The advices' precedence is also extremely important.

13

Static Crosscutting

As we have seen in several preceding chapters, advices can drastically change the runtime behavior of the affected classes. The static crosscutting features of the AspectJ tool discussed in this chapter enable you to change the object's static structure—from new data fields to different class hierarchies.

Test Case

To illustrate the examples of the static crosscutting we need a test case, as usual. The idea is to change the structure of this test class beyond recognition and let the class tell us all about it. Listing 13.1 shows the starting point.

LISTING 13.1   `SCMain.java` Class

```java
import java.util.*;

public class SCMain
{
    public static final String cvs="$Id$";

    public static void main(String args[])
    {
        SCMain sc = new SCMain();
        Class scClass = sc.getClass();

        printArray("Constructors: ", scClass.getConstructors()    );
        printArray("Interfaces:   ", scClass.getInterfaces()      );
        printArray("Fields:       ", scClass.getDeclaredFields() );
        printArray("Methods:      ", scClass.getDeclaredMethods());
        printArray("Parents:      ", getHierarchy(scClass));
    }

    private static void printArray(String title, Object[] array)
    {
        System.out.println(title);
        for(int i=0; i<array.length; i++)
        {
            System.out.println("  "+array[i]);
        }
    }

    private static Object[] getHierarchy(Class aClass)
    {
        ArrayList result = new ArrayList();
        Class superClass = aClass;

        do
        {
            result.add(superClass);
            superClass = superClass.getSuperclass();
        }
        while(null != superClass);

        return result.toArray();
    }
}
```

As you can probably tell, there is serious self-reflection going on—the class needs to describe its own structure after static modifications are applied. The main() method creates an instance of the class, and then calls various methods from the Java's reflection API. These methods return arrays of objects that describe components of the class: methods, fields, constructors, and interfaces. The utility method printArray() just prints out arrays of objects heavily relying on their implicitly provided toString() methods. Another utility method—getHierarchy() —creates an array of the object's ancestors.

To compile and execute the examples in this chapter the following commands can be used:

```
>ajc SCMain.java SCXXX.java
>java SCMain
```

In this code snippet, SCXXX stands for whatever concrete aspect are compiled with the SCMain class.

When this class is run alone, that is, without any aspects, it produces the following:

```
Constructors:
  public SCMain()
Interfaces:
Fields:
  public static final java.lang.String SCMain.cvs
Methods:
  public static void SCMain.main(java.lang.String[])
  private static void SCMain.printArray(java.lang.String,java.lang.Object[])
  private static java.lang.Object[] SCMain.getHierarchy(java.lang.Class)
Parents:
  class SCMain
  class java.lang.Object
```

In other words, our test class SCMain prints all there is to know about its structure, and literally, it all means this:

- The only constructor available is the default one generated by the compiler.

- There are no interfaces that this class implements.

- The methods are those explicitly defined in the code, that is, main(), printArray(), and getHierarchy().

- The class SCMain is an immediate descendant of the Object.

Although the following discussion concentrates on a single class SCMain created for the illustration purposes, the static crosscutting can be used on several classes simultaneously (this is why it is called crosscutting and not just "messing with the class structures"). This can be achieved by replacing class name SCMain with a type pattern as appropriate.

Field Introduction

Any aspect can add new fields to any other class using the following declaration:

```
[modifiers] TypePattern.Id [= expression]
```

In this declaration optional modifiers are either access modifiers, which are discussed later in this chapter, or storage type modifiers (final, static, transient, volatile). The field can be assigned an initial value by providing an optional initial-ization expression.

Let's consider an aspect that introduces new fields:

```
public aspect SCField
{
    public static int SCMain.publicStaticInt = 5;
    private String SCMain.privateString;
    volatile String SCMain.defaultString;
}
```

After compiling and running it with SCMain class, the latter recognizes these fields as its own:

```
Constructors:
  public SCMain()
Interfaces:
Fields:
  public static final java.lang.String SCMain.cvs
  public static int SCMain.publicStaticInt
  private java.lang.String SCMain.privateString_SCField
  volatile java.lang.String SCMain.defaultString_null
Methods:
  public static void SCMain.main(java.lang.String[])
  private static void SCMain.printArray(java.lang.String,java.lang.Object[])
  private static java.lang.Object[] SCMain.getHierarchy(java.lang.Class)
Parents:
  class SCMain
  class java.lang.Object
```

How did that happen? Well, no magic was involved—the AspectJ compiler simply inserted newly introduced fields into the code for the resulting SCMain class (see

Listing 13.2, which was produced using the -preprocess compilation flag. Note, repeated code fragments are omitted).

LISTING 13.2 Preprocessed SCMain.java Class

```java
import java.util.*;

public class SCMain
{
    public static final String cvs = "$Id$";
    public static void main(String[] args)
    {
        ...
    }

    private static void printArray(String title, Object[] array)
    {
        ...
    }

    private static Object[] getHierarchy(Class aClass)
    {
        ...
    }

    public static int publicStaticInt;
    private String privateString_SCField;
    volatile String defaultString_null;

    public SCMain()
    {
        super();
    }
    static
    {
        SCMain.publicStaticInt = 5;
    }
}
```

As you may have noticed, the generated fields' names are different from those declared in the SCField aspect. The ajc compiler does this to enforce access rules; this is discussed in detail later in the section "Access Rules and Privileged Aspects."

A similar approach is used for other kinds of member introduction—for methods and constructors (see the following section).

Method Introduction

Methods can be introduced in a similar fashion:

```
[abstract] [modifiers] Type TypePattern.Id(FormalParameters) { body }
```

Here, `modifiers` are access modifiers, `Type` is the method's return type, and `body` is a method's implementation code. An abstract method can be introduced but, obviously, the `TypePattern` must match only abstract classes. If the `TypePattern` includes interfaces, they will also begin supporting the new method.

The following aspect introduces two new methods:

```
public aspect SCMethod
{
    public static String SCMain.publicStaticVoid(String a, int b)
    {
        return a+b;
    }

    private int SCMain.privateInt(int a)
    {
        return a;
    }
}
```

And, the `SCMain` class promptly recognizes them:

```
Constructors:
  public SCMain()
Interfaces:
Fields:
  public static final java.lang.String SCMain.cvs
Methods:
  public static void SCMain.main(java.lang.String[])
  private static void SCMain.printArray(java.lang.String,java.lang.Object[])
  private static java.lang.Object[] SCMain.getHierarchy(java.lang.Class)
  public static java.lang.String SCMain.publicStaticVoid(java.lang.String,int)
  public int SCMain.privateInt_SCMethod(int)
Parents:
  class SCMain
  class java.lang.Object
```

Again, the generated member names have been changed here by the compiler as was mentioned previously.

Constructor Introduction

Constructor introduction is patterned after the method introduction, but the following exceptions apply: A constructor cannot be introduced to an interface and, of course, it cannot be declared abstract. Here is the syntax:

```
[modifiers] TypePattern.new(FormalParameters) { body }
```

This aspect introduces two new constructors:

```
public aspect SCConstructor
{
    public SCMain.new(String a)
    {
    }

    public SCMain.new()
    {
    }
}
```

The original intent was to introduce just SCMain(String) constructor, but after seeing it, the ajc did not generate a default constructor, which is used in the SCMain.main() method and which was generated automatically by the Java compiler (see Listing 13.1). So, the new explicit default constructor SCMain() had to be provided. Here is the proof that it worked and the SCMain class now has two constructors:

```
Constructors:
    public SCMain(java.lang.String)
    public SCMain()
Interfaces:
Fields:
    public static final java.lang.String SCMain.cvs
Methods:
    public static void SCMain.main(java.lang.String[])
    private static void SCMain.printArray(java.lang.String,java.lang.Object[])
    private static java.lang.Object[] SCMain.getHierarchy(java.lang.Class)
Parents:
    class SCMain
    class java.lang.Object
```

Access Rules and Privileged Aspects

As was described previously, the introduced fields, methods, and constructors can have access modifiers. Several rules govern how the access modifiers can be used:

- The protected access modifier is not supported.

- The default access to the introduced member is Java's default access; that is, package protected.

- All access rules are defined per introducing aspect, not per target class of the introduction.

For example, if a private method is introduced, it is private to the aspect that defines it—no other code is aware of it, including the class to which the method is declared to belong. Similarly, if aspect PackageA.aspectX introduces a field with the default access to a class PackageB.classY, the field will have a package protected access in PackageA only, and it will be totally invisible in PackageB. Consider the example in Listing 13.3.

LISTING 13.3   SCAccess.java Aspect

```
public aspect SCAccess
{
    public int SCMain.intPublic;
    private int SCMain.intPrivate;
    int SCMain.intDefault;

    public void SCMain.methodPublic()
    {
        this.methodPrivate();
    }

    private void SCMain.methodPrivate()
    {
    }

    void SCMain.methodDefault()
    {
    }

    public SCMain.new()
    {
    }
```

LISTING 13.3   Continued

```
    private SCMain.new(String a)
    {
    }

    SCMain.new(int a)
    {
    }
}
```

This aspect introduces three possible kinds of members (fields, methods, constructors) with all three kinds of access modifiers (public, private, default—also known as package protected) to the SCMain class. The class SCAccessTest (see Listing 13.4) tries to make use of them (note that all three entities—SCMain class, SCAccess aspect, and SCAccessTest class—belong to the same nameless package).

LISTING 13.4   SCAccessTest.java Class

```
public class SCAccessTest
{
    void test()
    {
        SCMain sc1 = new SCMain();
//      SCMain sc2 = new SCMain("aaa");
        SCMain sc3 = new SCMain(15);

        sc1.methodPublic();
        sc1.methodDefault();
//      sc1.methodPrivate();

        sc1.intPublic  = 5;
        sc1.intDefault = 5;
//      sc1.intPrivate = 5;
    }
}
```

The commented-out lines cannot be compiled because their corresponding members are declared private—private to the aspect SCAccess, that is. If the SCAccess is moved to another package by, say, making the following declaration

```
package aaa;
```

in the SCAccess.java file, the attempt to compile all three entities together results in the following output:

```
SCAccessTest.java:18:22:  SCMain(int) has package access
        SCMain sc3 = new SCMain(15);
                        ^

SCAccessTest.java:21:9:  void SCMain.methodDefault()
                                    from SCAccess has package access
        sc1.methodDefault();
        ^

SCAccessTest.java:25:13: SCMain.intDefault from SCAccess has package access
        sc1.intDefault = 5;
            ^

3 errors
```

This means the SCAccessTest class cannot access package-protected members of SCMain because they were introduced by the aspect aaa.SCAccess. Package protection covers the SCAccess package aaa, but not the nameless package to which SCAccessTest and SCMain happen to belong.

It is a worthwhile exercise to examine what kind of output SCMain produces with an SCAccess aspect that belongs to the same package or to a different one (SCAccessTest is not compiled with those two anymore).

The output with the SCAccess aspect is as follows:

```
Constructors:
  public SCMain()
  public SCMain(int,SCAccess)
  public SCMain(java.lang.String,SCAccess)
Interfaces:
Fields:
  public static final java.lang.String SCMain.cvs
  public int SCMain.intPublic
  private int SCMain.intPrivate_SCAccess
  int SCMain.intDefault_null
Methods:
  public static void SCMain.main(java.lang.String[])
  private static void SCMain.printArray(java.lang.String,java.lang.Object[])
  private static java.lang.Object[] SCMain.getHierarchy(java.lang.Class)
  public void SCMain.methodPublic()
  public void SCMain.methodPrivate_SCAccess()
  public void SCMain.methodDefault_null()
Parents:
```

```
class SCMain
class java.lang.Object
```

And here's the output with the aaa.SCAccess aspect:

```
Constructors:
  public SCMain()
  public SCMain(int,aaa.SCAccess)
  public SCMain(java.lang.String,aaa.SCAccess)
Interfaces:
Fields:
  public static final java.lang.String SCMain.cvs
  public int SCMain.intPublic
  private int SCMain.intPrivate_aaa_SCAccess
  int SCMain.intDefault_aaa
Methods:
  public static void SCMain.main(java.lang.String[])
  private static void SCMain.printArray(java.lang.String,java.lang.Object[])
  private static java.lang.Object[] SCMain.getHierarchy(java.lang.Class)
  public void SCMain.methodPublic()
  public void SCMain.methodPrivate_aaa_SCAccess()
  public void SCMain.methodDefault_aaa()
Parents:
  class SCMain
  class java.lang.Object
```

The members that are private to SCAccess aspect are qualified with the suffix
_SCAccess (field intPivate, method methodPrivate), and constructor
SCMain(String) is given a hidden special parameter of SCAccess type—and, of
course, only the aspect itself knows about it. The AspectJ compiler qualifies package-
protected members with package names—either null or aaa, which are also known
only to the aspect-controlled members of the same package.

Introducing new members to existing classes is prone to naming conflicts. If a type
pattern matches a class that already has a member with the name we are trying to
introduce, then it most likely will be an error. Most likely, of course, does not mean
always. For example, if we try to introduce a private member to a class that already
has a private member by the same name, nothing bad happens. The scopes of these
two will be separated and limited to the defining aspect and targeted class, respectively (unless the aspect is privileged, it is discussed below). The same is true for
package-protected members that belong to different packages. There are no name
conflicts if members' respective scopes do not intersect. Table 13.1 lists the name-
conflict rules.

Access Modifier	Same Package	Different Packages
private	OK	OK
default	Bad	OK
public	Bad	Bad

Sometimes, it is desired (but strongly advised against) for an aspect to be able to access private or protected members of a targeted class. ApsectJ allows this to happen if the aspect is declared `privileged`. It, obviously, allows for breaking the conflict resolution rules described in Table 13.1. In the case of privileged aspects, the conflict resolution should follow an additional implicit rule: A member that would be visible if the aspect was not `privileged` must take precedence.

Consider the following example. The class `SCClass.java` declares a private variable a:

```
public class  SCClass
{
    private int a=1;
}
```

The aspect `SCPrivileged.java` introduces a new field a:

```
public aspect SCPrivileged
{
    private int SCClass.a=2;

    public static void main(String args[])
    {
        System.out.println(new SCClass().a);
    }
}
```

Because both fields (aspect's and class's) are private, there is no conflict. When these two files compiled together and `SCPrivileged` is executed, it prints out 2. Let's change the aspect's declaration to become privileged:

```
public privileged aspect SCPrivileged
{
    private int SCClass.a=2;

    public static void main(String args[])
    {
        System.out.println(new SCClass().a);
    }
}
```

Then an attempt to compile it with SCClass causes the conflict, which is flagged by the compiler:

```
SCPrivileged.java:12:5: SCClass.a from SCPrivileged conflicts with SCClass.a:
➡introduced member
    private int SCClass.a=2;
    ^

1 errors
```

The only explanation I have is that the precedence rule with regard to privileged aspects has not been implemented yet.

Extension

In addition to introducing new members, AspectJ enables you to introduce a class to a completely new set of parent classes, thus, changing a static class hierarchy. The syntax for such introduction is

```
declare parents: TypePattern extends ParentTypeList;
```

In this example, TypePattern specifies targeted classes, and ParentTypeList declares the parent types (there can be several, but all must belong to the same hierarchy). Let's make the example SCMain.java class something else—let's convert it from just an Object to an Exception:

```
public aspect SCParent
{
    declare parents: SCMain extends IllegalThreadStateException;
}
```

In this aspect, the introduction can also be written as

```
    declare parents: SCMain extends Object, IllegalThreadStateException, Exception;
```

with identical results:

```
Constructors:
  public SCMain()
Interfaces:
Fields:
  public static final java.lang.String SCMain.cvs
Methods:
  public static void SCMain.main(java.lang.String[])
  private static void SCMain.printArray(java.lang.String,java.lang.Object[])
```

```
    private static java.lang.Object[] SCMain.getHierarchy(java.lang.Class)
Parents:
  class SCMain
  class java.lang.IllegalThreadStateException
  class java.lang.IllegalArgumentException
  class java.lang.RuntimeException
  class java.lang.Exception
  class java.lang.Throwable
  class java.lang.Object
```

The last section of the output (`Parents:`) clearly shows that `SCMain` is now an `IllegalThreadStateException`.

Implementation

If introducing new parents is not enough, an arbitrary class can be forced to implement new interfaces (one or several):

```
declare parents: TypePattern implements InterfaceTypeList;
```

where `TypePattern` specifies targeted classes and `InterfaceTypeList` declares the interface types that must be implemented by the class. The example `SCInterface.java` follows:

```
public aspect SCInterface
{
    declare parents: SCMain implements Comparable;

    public int SCMain.compareTo(Object o)
    {
        return this.hashCode() - o.hashCode();
    }
}
```

By virtue of this aspect, instances of the class `SCMain` can now be compared. Of course, the implementation of the introduced interface must be present some-where—either in the targeted class (if it is already there) or in the introducing aspect as in the previous example. The class `SCMain` now readily admits to being compara-ble (that it implements the `Comparable` interface):

```
Constructors:
  public SCMain()
Interfaces:
```

```
  interface java.lang.Comparable
Fields:
  public static final java.lang.String SCMain.cvs
Methods:
  public static void SCMain.main(java.lang.String[])
  public int SCMain.compareTo(java.lang.Object)
  private static void SCMain.printArray(java.lang.String,java.lang.Object[])
  private static java.lang.Object[] SCMain.getHierarchy(java.lang.Class)
Parents:
  class SCMain
  class java.lang.Object
```

Warnings and Errors

The AspectJ compiler provides a facility that can detect some pointcuts statically (that is, at compile time) and issue a warning or error. A warning instructs the compiler to print out a text message and continue compilation, whereas an error makes the compiler print the message and quit. The syntax is as follows:

```
declare warning : Pointcut : String;
declare error : Pointcut : String;
```

In this syntax, String is the message to be printed by the compiler, and Pointcut is a statically determinable pointcut. Such pointcuts pick join points that are, in this situation, places in the source code that correspond to some real join points when the program is executing. Because there is no runtime context at the compile time, the statically determinable pointcuts must not be, and cannot be, expressed in terms of the following primitive pointcuts that depend on runtime information to work:

```
this
target
args
cflow
cflowbelow
if
```

This SCWarning.java aspect produces the warning if a SCMain's constructor is called:

```
public aspect SCWarning
{
    declare warning: call(SCMain.new(..)) : "Constructor called!";
}
```

Its compilation output is as follows:

```
SCMain.java:21:21: Constructor called! (warning)
        SCMain sc = new SCMain();
```

When executed, SCMain with SCWarning aspect produces output identical to that presented for SCMain at the beginning of the chapter. The SCWarning aspect does not have any runtime effects.

The SCError aspect stops the compilation of the program when SCMain's constructor is encountered and issues the error message:

```
public aspect SCError
{
    declare error: execution(SCMain.new(..)) : "Constructor executed!";
}
```

Its compilation output is as follows:

```
SCMain.java:15:1: Constructor executed!
public class SCMain
^
1 errors
```

No other output, naturally, follows, and the process stops right here.

Softened Exceptions

It is extremely convenient to be able to mute Java's exceptions at some points. The AspectJ provides such capability in a form of softened exceptions:

```
declare soft: TypePattern : Pointcut;
```

Here, TypePattern describes exceptions to be softened, and Pointcut is a statically determinable pointcut (all restrictions described in the previous section, apply here as well) that picks the places in the code where the softening should happen.

The softening means that the AspectJ will find all places specified by the pointcut and catch the exceptions that match the TypePattern. They will be wrapped in org.aspectj.lang.SoftException and the latter will be rethrown. Because the SoftException is a subclass of the RuntimException, the Java's static exception checking will, therefore, be circumvented. Consider the example SCSoftException aspect:

```
public aspect SCSoftException
{
```

```
        declare soft: IllegalAccessException : call(SCMain.new(..));
}
```

The aspect is going to soften an IllegalAccessException for all calls to SCMain's constructors. Because they do not throw anything, we have to modify SCConstructor aspect to provide one to throw what we need:

```
public SCMain.new() throws IllegalAccessException
{
    throw new IllegalAccessException();
}
```

If we try to compile the new version of the SCConstructor aspect with the SCMain class, the compile time error will result:

```
public SCMain.new() throws IllegalAccessException
```

```
SCMain.java:21:21: unreported exception java.lang.IllegalAccessException;
        must be caught or declared to be thrown
        SCMain sc = new SCMain();
                    ^
```

```
1 errors
```

When the SCSoftException is added to the compilation list, the whole thing compiles smoothly and produces the following output:

```
org.aspectj.lang.SoftException
        at SCMain.new$constructor_call(SCMain.java;SCConstructor.java(1k);
                SCSoftException.java(2k):2014)
        at SCMain.main(SCMain.java;SCConstructor.java(1k);
                SCSoftException.java(2k):20)
```

This means, the softened exception is propagated until the main() method of SCMain class terminates the running thread.

Summary

In this chapter we considered the static crosscutting features of the AspectJ language. This concludes the description of the language itself. Chapter 14, "Use Patterns," will describe several popular use patterns.

PART IV

Conclusion

IN THIS PART

"And how many hours a day did you do lessons?" said Alice, in a
hurry to change the subject.

"Ten hours the first day," said the Mock Turtle: "nine the next, and
so on."

"What a curious plan!" exclaimed Alice.

"That's the reason they're called lessons," the Gryphon remarked:
"because they lessen from day to day."

—Lewis Carroll, *Alice's Adventures in Wonderland*, Chapter IX

In the final part of the book we will discuss emerging use
patterns, and I'll make some concluding remarks.

14

Use Patterns

The "Gang-of-Four" book (*Design Patterns: Elements of Reusable Object-Oriented Software*; see Appendix F, "References") created a very active cottage industry devoted to patternizing everything, and for a good reason—people like to classify, categorize, and dissect for the sake of knowledge accumulation. A search for books about design patterns produces about 400 matches of titles in print and, conservatively assuming that half of them are related to programming and not to textile and quilts, that is a staggering number. The aspirations of this book are far more modest: The AOP industry is still in its infancy, and true design patterns tend to emerge after people repeatedly use similar solutions to solve similar problems over some time. There is no doubt that AOP-related patterns will fill some very thick books in the future, but for now the sheer number of developers using AspectJ is not nearly sufficient to produce repeating solutions.

Nevertheless, the people participating in the AspectJ mailing list discussions (about 700 subscribers in April 2002) managed to come up with some stable idioms that eventually made it to the AspectJ's FAQ list. These idioms are not strictly design patterns as described in the "Gang-of-Four" book meaning, "descriptions of communicating objects and classes that are customized to solve a general design problem in a particular context." There are rather encouraging signs of an emerging usage tradition that grows with the popularity of AspectJ. As such, in this book they are called usage patterns, and they do show how to use AspectJ better and how to avoid common beginner's mistakes.

The list of usage patterns that follows is nowhere near exhaustive. The goal is to provide the flavor of them and tease the developers of the world to come. More usage patterns are available in AspectJ FAQ lists and users' archives (see Appendix E, "AspectJ Project," for details).

Shooting Yourself in the Tail

One of the first experiences with AspectJ can be quite negative. The simplest aspect that is designed to trace calls and provide the wealth of information about everything you ever call causes a stack overflow instead. Consider one such aspect, PtrnUnlimitedRecursion:

```
public aspect PtrnUnlimitedRecursion
{
    pointcut p() : call(* *.*(..));

    before() : p()
    {
        System.out.println(thisJoinPoint);
    }
}
```

The intent of this aspect is, obviously, to trace all method calls made anywhere in the program. When compiled and executed with the following main PtrnUnlimitedRecursionMain class (which is also very simple):

```
public class PtrnUnlimitedRecursionMain
{
    public static void main(String args[])
    {
        System.out.println("*** Inside main ***");
    }
}
```

the following problem results:

```
java.lang.StackOverflowError
        at PtrnUnlimitedRecursion.before0$ajc(PtrnUnlimitedRecursion.java:19)
        at PtrnUnlimitedRecursion.println$method_call(PtrnUnlimitedRecursion.java)
        at PtrnUnlimitedRecursion.before0$ajc(PtrnUnlimitedRecursion.java:19)
        at PtrnUnlimitedRecursion.println$method_call(PtrnUnlimitedRecursion.java)
        at PtrnUnlimitedRecursion.before0$ajc(PtrnUnlimitedRecursion.java:19)
        at PtrnUnlimitedRecursion.println$method_call(PtrnUnlimitedRecursion.java)
        at PtrnUnlimitedRecursion.before0$ajc(PtrnUnlimitedRecursion.java:19)

        ...
```

It looks like methods before0$ajc() and println$method_call()of the compiled aspect PtrnUnlimitedRecursion call each other recursively and indefinitely. Indeed, the source of the compiled aspect reveals the problem in all its glory:

```
public class PtrnUnlimitedRecursion
{
    ...

    public final void before0$ajc(org.aspectj.lang.JoinPoint thisJoinPoint)
    {
        this.println$method_call(System.out, thisJoinPoint);
    }

    ...

    private void println$method_call(java.io.PrintStream target,
                                                    final Object __0)
    {
        ...
        if (PtrnUnlimitedRecursion.hasAspect())
            PtrnUnlimitedRecursion.aspect$.before0$ajc(thisJoinPoint);

        target.println(__0);
    }

    ...
}
```

Because the aspect PtrnUnlimitedRecursion can and does advise itself, the call System.out.println() is also advised, thus creating an unlimited recursion. The remedy is simple and it has been seen on several occasions throughout the book— tell the advice not to advise itself:

```
public aspect PtrnUnlimitedRecursion
{
    pointcut p() : call(* *.*(..));

    before() : p() && !within(PtrnUnlimitedRecursion)
    {
        System.out.println(thisJoinPoint);
    }
}
```

And it produces rather predictable output:

```
call(void java.io.PrintStream.println(String))
*** Inside main ***
```

Of course, it would be really tempting to keep the suspense about these mysterious `!within(something)` pointcuts up to this point, but the idiom is so prevailing that it was absolutely impossible. Nevertheless, about every other month the question regarding the stack overflow problems comes up in the AspectJ user mailing list, and it is usually connected to some variant of the case presented previously—a pointcut crosscuts more than intended. It is typically a normal mistake made by people just joining ranks of AspectJ users, and it has been rightfully nominated as the most frequently asked question.

We Want It All

Because we have been burned before with pointcuts that pick more than needed, it is highly desirable to find out what join points are there and, therefore, available for picking. The following `PtrnJPAll` aspect prints them all:

```
public aspect PtrnJPAll
{
    pointcut p() : if(true);

    before() : p() && !within(PtrnJPAll)
    {
        System.out.println(thisJoinPoint);
    }
}
```

The aspect contains the pointcut `if(true)`, which is the simplest pointcut I could create. Because the logical condition is always true, all possible join points are included. Naturally, we want to exclude the `before()` advice from advising itself by the virtue of ever-present `!within()` pointcut. Here is the `PtrnJPMain` program to be advised:

```
public class PtrnJPMain
{
    public void test()
    {
        System.out.println("*** Inside test ***");
    }

    public static void main(String args[])
```

```
    {
        System.out.println("*** Calling test ***");
        new PtrnJPMain().test();
    }
}
```

When executed with the previous aspect, it produces the following output:

```
staticinitialization(PtrnJPMain.<init>)
execution(void PtrnJPMain.main(String[]))
get(PrintStream java.lang.System.out)
call(void java.io.PrintStream.println(String))
*** Calling test ***
call(PtrnJPMain())
initialization(PtrnJPMain())
execution(PtrnJPMain.<init>)
execution(PtrnJPMain())
call(void PtrnJPMain.test())
execution(void PtrnJPMain.test())
get(PrintStream java.lang.System.out)
call(void java.io.PrintStream.println(String))
*** Inside test ***
```

And it indeed represents the full roster of join points in existence for the program PtrnJPMain. For a 10-line program the aspect discovered 12 join points, but for any real program the count quickly reaches millions. It is possible to limit the number of picked join points if the previous advice starts executing at some point of the program and stops when another point is reached. Naturally, these points can be picked by specially constructed pointcuts. Consider the following PtrnJPSelected aspect:

```
public aspect PtrnJPSelected
{
    pointcut begin() : execution(* *.main(..));
    pointcut end()   : execution(void PtrnJPMain.test());

    pointcut p() : cflow(begin()) && !cflowbelow(end());

    before() : p() && !within(PtrnJPSelected)
    {
        System.out.println(thisJoinPoint);
    }
}
```

Here the workhorse pointcut p() is expressed in terms of previously defined point-cuts begin() and end(). It means the following: Pick all join points that belong to the control flow of begin(), but not below the control flow of the end(). As such, p() creates a band of join points encountered between certain join points specified by begin() and end() pointcuts. In this example, the band is between execution of main() and test() methods of PtrnJPMain class:

```
execution(void PtrnJPMain.main(String[]))
get(PrintStream java.lang.System.out)
call(void java.io.PrintStream.println(String))
*** Calling test ***
call(PtrnJPMain())
initialization(PtrnJPMain())
execution(PtrnJPMain.<init>)
execution(PtrnJPMain())
call(void PtrnJPMain.test())
execution(void PtrnJPMain.test())
*** Inside test ***
```

It so happens that on this execution path there are only nine join points. The p() pointcut can be further qualified to include only join points in particular classes or on particular targets.

Following the Recursion Path

Recursive calls can be quite useful when they are not causing problems. Consider the following PtrnRecursiveCallsMain program:

```
public class PtrnRecursiveCallsMain
{
    public static void main(String args[])
    {
        try
        {
            printParents(Class.forName(args[0]));
        }
        catch(Exception e)
        {
            System.out.println(e);
        }
    }

    static void printParents(Class o)
```

```
    {
        if( null == o )
        {
            return;
        }

        System.out.println(" *** "+o.getName()+" *** ");
        printParents(o.getSuperclass());
    }
}
```

It prints out a class hierarchy for the class given as its argument. For example, for the class java.lang.Integer it produces the following:

```
*** java.lang.Integer ***
*** java.lang.Number ***
*** java.lang.Object ***
```

The method printParents() is a recursive version of method SCMain.getHierarchy() presented earlier.

Advising recursive methods can be quite counterproductive because they are executed so many times and, thus, contain a lot of repeating join points. Most interesting of them all are, of course, the first and the last calls of the recursion. Consider the following PtrnRecursiveCalls aspect:

```
public aspect PtrnRecursiveCalls
{
    pointcut every() : call(void PtrnRecursiveCallsMain.printParents(Class));
    pointcut first() : every() && !cflowbelow(every());

    before() : every()
    {
        System.out.println("Every: "+thisJoinPoint);
    }

    before() : first()
    {
        System.out.println("First: "+thisJoinPoint);
    }
}
```

The pointcut every() picks every call to the printParents() method. The pointcut first() picks only the first one, and its body can be read as every call to `printParents()` that is not under the `printParents()` control flow. Of course, the same pointcut can be written, albeit far less elegant and general, as

```
pointcut first() : every() && !withincode(void *.printParents(Class));
```

If `printParents()` has to call itself for reasons unrelated to its main recursion, this first call will never be picked. It will also limit the reusability of the `first()` point-cut—with `cflow` it is expressed only it terms of other pointcut `every()`—and is not dependent on any particular class or method.

Compiling the example with the aspect produces the following:

```
Every: call(void PtrnRecursiveCallsMain.printParents(Class))
First: call(void PtrnRecursiveCallsMain.printParents(Class))
 *** java.lang.Integer ***
Every: call(void PtrnRecursiveCallsMain.printParents(Class))
 *** java.lang.Number ***
Every: call(void PtrnRecursiveCallsMain.printParents(Class))
 *** java.lang.Object ***
Every: call(void PtrnRecursiveCallsMain.printParents(Class))
```

The second `before()` advice executes only once; before the first call to the `printParents()` method.

The other desired pointcut—the one that picks the last call of the recursion—represents a problem. Intuitively, it sounds easy: Pick calls to `printParents()` that do not contain other `printParents()` in their control flow. I was, however, unable to express the idea in AspectJ and, thus, have to offer it as an exercise to the reader.

Getting in Synch

Sometimes it is highly desirable to synchronize certain code. Because the AspectJ language does not enable you to introduce synchronization, the following usage pattern is exercised. Consider the following `PtrnSynchronizationMain` class:

```
public class PtrnSynchronizationMain extends Thread
{
    static double r;
    static PtrnSynchronizationMain ps = new PtrnSynchronizationMain();

    void test()
    {
        double s = Math.random();
        r = s;
        System.out.println(s+" -> "+r);
    }
```

```
public void run()
{
    ps.test();
}

public static void main(String args[])
{
    for(int i=0; i<5; i++)
    {
        (new PtrnSynchronizationMain()).start();
    }
}
}
```

The program starts five concurrent threads that call method test() on a static object ps. The method generates a random double number and assigns it to the static field r. After that both values—generated and assigned—are printed. This is what happens when the program is executed by itself (without any aspects):

```
0.1368094516088577  -> 0.8809738862497517
0.5743913752760986  -> 0.8809738862497517
0.7922839875668042  -> 0.8809738862497517
0.8809738862497517  -> 0.8809738862497517
0.22426201780025357 -> 0.8809738862497517
```

(You might want to add some delay between the r=s; and System.out.println() statements to achieve more consistent results.)

The static field does not have the value of what was assigned because other threads constantly overwrite it. To synchronize the execution of the test() method, the PtrnSynchronization aspect can be written like this:

```
public aspect PtrnSynchronization
{
    pointcut p() : execution(void PtrnSynchronizationMain.test());

    Object around(Object o) : this(o) && p()
    {
        synchronized(o)
        {
            return proceed(o);
        }
    }
}
```

The around() advice synchronizes the execution of the test() method picked by the pointcut p(), using the executing object itself picked by this pointcut. In order for the whole scheme to work, it needs the parameter that represents the executing object. When this aspect is compiled and executed with the example program, the output changes to

```
0.6083253152913415    -> 0.6083253152913415
0.11495914746220903 -> 0.11495914746220903
0.32386044833410876 -> 0.32386044833410876
0.3898087079337521    -> 0.3898087079337521
0.2791895717783135    -> 0.2791895717783135
```

The execution of test() is now synchronized, and the static field retains its value.

Hyper-Cutting

As we discussed in Part I of this book, the regular Java objects and AspectJ's aspects create orthogonal hierarchies. The world is modeled in objects, and aspects crosscut the objects to provide modularity of concerns. But is it possible to crosscut aspects? What if there is some reusable functionality or concern that can be encapsulated (and, later on, reused) in an aspect? Such encapsulation can provide a "third dimension" to the objects-aspects space, thus, hyper-cutting crosscuts. There is no direct support for such a thing in the AspectJ language, but there is a hyper-cutting idiom that enables it to emulate aspects' remodularization. This remodularization is different from aspect inheritance—instead of extending aspect's behavior, it should make aspects crosscut class hierarchies according to an arbitrary criterion.

Consider the following PtrnHyper aspect:

```
public aspect PtrnHyper
{
    public interface Tag
    {
    }

    pointcut p() : execution(* Tag+.*(..));

    before() : p()
    {
        System.out.println(thisJoinPoint);
    }
}
```

This declares inner interface `Tag` and expresses its (aspect's) crosscutting behavior in terms of this interface—in this example the pointcut `p()` picks executions of all methods implementing `Tag`. Please note that `Tag+.*(..)` does not mean "all methods of interface `Tag`" (by the way, it does not have any); because type patterns and signature patterns are applied separately, it means "all methods of all classes that implement `Tag`." So far, there are no classes implementing `Tag` interface. but that could change! Consider the following two test classes.

The `PtrnHyperMain.java` class is as follows:

```
public class PtrnHyperMain
{
    public static void main(String args[])
    {
        PtrnHyperTest ht = new PtrnHyperTest();
        ht.test();
    }
}
```

And this is the `PtrnHyperTest.java` class:

```
public class PtrnHyperTest
{
    void test()
    {
    }
}
```

If we want to "apply" the `PtrnHyper` aspect to any class whatsoever, we need to introduce that class to the `Tag` interface. Here's the `PtrnHyperApply` aspect:

```
public aspect PtrnHyperApply
{
    declare parents: PtrnHyperMain implements PtrnHyper.Tag;
    declare parents: PtrnHyperTest implements PtrnHyper.Tag;
}
```

If these four pieces of source code are compiled and executed together, the class `PtrnHyperMain` produces the following output:

```
execution(void PtrnHyperMain.main(String[]))
execution(void PtrnHyperTest.test())
```

If the second introduction in aspect `PtrnHyperApply` is commented out, the output changes to

```
execution(void PtrnHyperMain.main(String[]))
```

Thus, the `PtrnHyperApply` aspect can selectively make `PtrnHyper` aspect applicable to a varying number of classes depending on the need. Of course, any number of other aspects that introduce the `Tag` interface to any more classes can be created, thus, reusing the `PtrnHyper` code for classes it was never aware of, meaning, the classes it does not crosscut directly. The main advantage of hyper-cutting over the simple abstract pointcut approach is that the original aspect's pointcuts can be reused as long as they are expressed in terms of some third-dimension interface.

A Word of Caution

Now that you've seen how aspect-oriented programming works, a word of caution is in order. The crosscutting features of the AspectJ tool are powerful, challenging, and interesting, which also makes them quite dangerous. They give you power to change existing code in ways that the original design did not intend. Before suitable design methodologies that account for crosscutting emerge, AspectJ probably will be used most often in already existing systems. I wish I had a recipe on how to avoid trouble with aspects all the time, but I do not—you have to exercise your judgment.

Besides philosophical difficulties, some practical ones require additional attention:

- As we emphasized several times already, AspectJ requires access to all the source code that aspects are intended to affect. In practical terms it means that for any real program several hundred or several thousand classes (depending on what *real program* means to you) need to be compiled in one go on every change no matter how minor. It is a very slow process. The developers of AspectJ are keenly aware of this fact and, reportedly, an incremental compiler is in the works. In the meantime, the only useful strategy is segmentation of the source code into more or less independent sections to be compiled separately, which limits the reach of your aspects.

- It has been announced that future versions of the AspectJ compiler will support crosscutting using byte codes, meaning, the source code will not be required. It will provide more power to you with a corresponding increase in the chances of shooting yourself in the foot. It would be really worrisome if someone on the development team was able to advise the Java runtime library at will. Hopefully, some safeguards will be developed along with the new compiler.

- It is not at all clear how the reusable libraries of aspects can be shrink-wrapped and distributed. Currently, they are required to be in the source code form to work. Additionally, if a third-party library uses aspects, the AspectJ runtime library should be included into the distribution. If the library relies on crosscutting in its functionality, the target source, obviously, needs to be compiled with AspectJ.

I hope that these points do no sound discouraging—like any leading edge technology, AspectJ has to mature to enter the mainstream, and to mature it has to be used!

This concludes the description of the AspectJ language and its compiler. As you've seen, the use patterns are developing fast, and the members of the AspectJ users mailing list are a very attentive audience to which you can submit your own pattern ideas.

The appendixes that follow this chapter contain some auxiliary information that did not find its place in the main text, but which is nevertheless deemed to be worthy of your attention.

On a final note, good luck! I hope that the book has changed your perspective on the future of programming, and that you are willing to help bring this future a little closer.

A

AspectJ API

AspectJ comes with two packages in its published API: org.aspectj.lang and org.aspectj.lang.reflect. Instead of reproducing the full autogenerated set of API documentation (it comes with the distribution), we will concentrate on the parts that are most frequently used.

Listing A.1 shows the full hierarchy of the API.

LISTING A.1   The Hierarchy of AspectJ-Published API

```
Classes
class java.lang.Object
  class java.lang.Throwable
    class java.lang.Exception
      class java.lang.RuntimeException
        class org.aspectj.lang.MultipleAspectsBoundException
        class org.aspectj.lang.NoAspectBoundException
        class org.aspectj.lang.SoftException

Interfaces
interface org.aspectj.lang.JoinPoint
interface org.aspectj.lang.JoinPoint.StaticPart
interface org.aspectj.lang.Signature
  interface org.aspectj.lang.reflect.CatchClauseSignature
  interface org.aspectj.lang.reflect.MemberSignature
    interface org.aspectj.lang.reflect.CodeSignature
      interface org.aspectj.lang.reflect.AdviceSignature
      interface org.aspectj.lang.reflect.ConstructorSignature
      interface org.aspectj.lang.reflect.InitializerSignature
      interface org.aspectj.lang.reflect.MethodSignature
    interface org.aspectj.lang.reflect.FieldSignature
interface org.aspectj.lang.reflect.SourceLocation
```

Interfaces `JoinPoint` and `JoinPoint.StaticPart`

The AspectJ compiler creates and provides two special variables to an advice for each join point encountered: `thisJoinPoint` and `thisJoinPointStaticPart`. These variables have the types that implement `org.aspectj.lang.JoinPoint` and `org.aspectj.lang.JoinPoint.StaticPart`, respectively. The latter contains reflection information about join points that does not depend on a runtime context, and if no runtime information is required by an advice, the use of `thisJoinPointStaticPart` is preferable because of its low runtime overhead.

`JoinPoint.StaticPart` Methods

The interface `org.aspectj.lang.JoinPoint.StaticPart` provides the following methods.

```
JoinPoint.StaticPart.getSignature
public Signature getSignature()
```

This method returns the signature at the join point. The interface Signature (see the following section for details) contains many useful methods to drill deeper into the pointcut structure.

JoinPoint.StaticPart.getSourceLocation
public SourceLocation getSourceLocation()

This method returns the source location where the join point is encountered or null if no location is available. The SourceLocation interface (see the section "Interface SourceLocation" for details) provides methods for locating the filename, and the line number for the join point.

JoinPoint.StaticPart.getKind
public java.lang.String getKind()

This method returns a join point's type in a String—such as method-execution, method-call, initialization, and so on.

JoinPoint.StaticPart.toString
public java.lang.String toString()

This method returns a String representation of this join point including its kind and signature. Something similar to the following for the call to Integer.parseInt(String) method:

call(int java.lang.Integer.parseInt(String))

JoinPoint.StaticPart.toShortString
public java.lang.String toShortString()

This method returns a terse version of the toString() output:

call(Integer.parseInt(..))

JoinPoint.StaticPart.toLongString
public java.lang.String toLongString()

This method returns a really verbose version of the toString() output:

call(public static int java.lang.Integer.parseInt(java.lang.String))

JoinPoint **Methods**

The interface org.aspectj.lang.JoinPoint implements all the methods of the org.aspectj.lang.JoinPoint.StaticPart and several runtime dependent methods.

```
JoinPoint.getThis
public java.lang.Object getThis()
```

This method returns the currently executing object if available, null if not.

```
JoinPoint.getTarget
public java.lang.Object getTarget()
```

This method returns the target object or null if the target is not available.

```
JoinPoint.getArgs
public java.lang.Object[] getArgs()
```

This method returns the arguments available at the join point or an empty array if no arguments are present. Primitive types are wrapped in their respective object wrappers.

Interface Signature **and Its Subinterfaces**

The interface org.aspectj.lang.Signature declares methods to describe the language construct at the join point—methods, fields, constructors, exceptions, and so on as shown in this hierarchy:

```
interface org.aspectj.lang.Signature
  interface org.aspectj.lang.reflect.CatchClauseSignature
  interface org.aspectj.lang.reflect.MemberSignature
    interface org.aspectj.lang.reflect.CodeSignature
      interface org.aspectj.lang.reflect.AdviceSignature
      interface org.aspectj.lang.reflect.ConstructorSignature
      interface org.aspectj.lang.reflect.InitializerSignature
      interface org.aspectj.lang.reflect.MethodSignature
    interface org.aspectj.lang.reflect.FieldSignature
```

Its subinterfaces (AdviceSignature, CatchClauseSignature, CodeSignature, ConstructorSignature, FieldSignature, InitializerSignature, MemberSignature, MethodSignature—all in package org.aspectj.lang.reflect) add methods relevant to the particular signature type.

Signature.toString, Signature.toShortString, and Signature.toLongString

```
public java.lang.String toString()
public java.lang.String toShortString()
public java.lang.String toLongString()
```

These methods return a string representation of the join point in a manner similar to their `JoinPoint.StaticPart` counterparts. For the `Integer.parseInt(String)` method, the string representation will be, respectively:

```
int java.lang.Integer.parseInt(String)
public static int java.lang.Integer.parseInt(java.lang.String)
Integer.parseInt(..)
```

Signature.getName

```
public java.lang.String getName()
```

This method returns the name (id) for the method or field. For example, for the `Integer.parseInt(String)` method, the returned name will be parseInt; for the field getters and setters for `Pcds.a` field, the name will be a. It returns an empty string when the name is not available, for example, in the case of the `CatchClauseSignature`.

Signature.getDeclaringType

```
public java.lang.Class getDeclaringType()
```

This method returns the `Class` object for the type that defines the signature: for example, `java.lang.Interger` for the `Integer.parseInt(String)` method.

CatchClauseSignature.getParameterType

```
public java.lang.Class getParameterType()
```

This method returns the `Class` object for the type and the catch clause for the handler execution join point.

CatchClauseSignature.getParameterName

```
public java.lang.String getParameterName()
```

This method returns the name of the parameter for the caught type.

CodeSignature.getParameterTypes

```
public java.lang.Class[] getParameterTypes()
```

This method returns `Class` objects for all the parameters of the signatures that represent methods, advices, constructors, and initializers (the `CodeSignature` interface is a parent interface for all of the previous).

CodeSignature.getParameterNames

```
public java.lang.String[] getParameterNames()
```

This method returns all the respective parameters' names for code signatures.

CodeSignature.getExceptionTypes

```
public java.lang.Class[] getExceptionTypes()
```

This method returns the types of exceptions that can be thrown at the join point described by the signature.

AdviceSignature.getReturnType

```
public java.lang.Class getReturnType()
```

This method returns the return type for the signature representing an advice.

MethodSignature.getReturnType

```
public java.lang.Class getReturnType()
```

This method returns the return type for the signature representing a method.

FieldSignature.getFieldType

```
public java.lang.Class getFieldType()
```

This method returns a `Class` object for the field that the current signature represents.

Interface SourceLocation

The interface `org.aspectj.lang.reflect.SourceLocation` declares methods to locate the physical position of a join point in the source code.

SourceLocation.getWithinType

```
public java.lang.Class getWithinType()
```

This method returns the Class object for the type where the corresponding join point happened to be encountered.

SourceLocation.getFileName

```
public java.lang.String getFileName()
```

This method returns the filename where the join point is located.

SourceLocation.getLine

```
public int getLine()
```

This method returns the line number in the file for the current join point.

SourceLocation.getColumn

```
public int getColumn()
```

This method returns the column number for the current join point.

Exceptions

The AspectJ API defines three runtime exceptions:

```
org.aspectj.lang.MultipleAspectsBoundException
org.aspectj.lang.NoAspectBoundException
org.aspectj.lang.SoftException
```

MultipleAspectsBoundException

This exception is not used in the current implementation.

NoAspectsBoundException

This exception is thrown from aspectOf() autogenerated methods for aspects declared perthis, pertarget, percflow, and percflowbelow.

SoftException

The `org.aspectj.lang.SoftEsception` is a wrapper exception designed to hold another exception that is to be "softened." The `SoftException` receives its content via constructor:

```
SoftException(java.lang.Throwable e)
```

The content can be accessed later by method

```
java.lang.Throwable getWrappedThrowable()
```

An Example

The example in Listing A.2 uses all the API described previously. Aspect `APIAspect` attempts to capture all join points in the source compiled with it and runs its `before()` advice to introspect them.

LISTING A.2   `APIAspect.java` Aspect

```
import org.aspectj.lang.*;
import org.aspectj.lang.reflect.*;

public aspect APIAspect
{
    pointcut p(): if(true);

    before() : p() && !within(APIAspect)
    {
        System.out.println("******* "+thisJoinPointStaticPart.toString()+
                                                       " *******");
        System.out.println("Target:        "+thisJoinPoint.getThis());
        System.out.println("This:          "+thisJoinPoint.getTarget());

        Object o[] = thisJoinPoint.getArgs();
        System.out.print("Arguments:      ");
        for(int i=0; i<o.length; i++ )
        {
            System.out.print(o[i].getClass().getName()+"("+o[i]+") ");
        }
        System.out.println();

        Signature sig = thisJoinPointStaticPart.getSignature();
        System.out.println("Signature:      "+sig.toString());
```

LISTING A.2 Continued

```
    System.out.println("Signature name: "+sig.getName());
    System.out.println("Declaring type: "+sig.getDeclaringType());

    if( sig instanceof CatchClauseSignature )
    {
        System.out.println("Signature type:    "+"CatchClause");
        System.out.println("   Param type:  "+
                    ((CatchClauseSignature) sig).getParameterType());
        System.out.println("   Param name:  "+
                    ((CatchClauseSignature) sig).getParameterName());
    }
    if( sig instanceof MemberSignature )
    {
        System.out.println("Signature type:    "+"Member");
    }
    if( sig instanceof CodeSignature )
    {
        System.out.println("Signature type:    "+"Code");

        Class  c[] = ((CodeSignature) sig).getParameterTypes();
        String s[] = ((CodeSignature) sig).getParameterNames();
        for(int i = 0; i<c.length; i++)
        {
            System.out.println("   Param type:   "+c[i]);
            System.out.println("   Param name:   "+s[i]);
        }

        Class  e[] = ((CodeSignature) sig).getExceptionTypes();
        for(int i = 0; i<e.length; i++)
        {
            System.out.println("   Exception type: "+e[i]);
        }

    }
    if( sig instanceof AdviceSignature )
    {
        System.out.println("Signature type:    "+"Advice");
        System.out.println("   Return type: "+
                        ((AdviceSignature) sig).getReturnType());
    }
    if( sig instanceof ConstructorSignature )
    {
```

LISTING A.2   Continued

```
            System.out.println("Signature type:    "+"Constructor");
        }
        if( sig instanceof InitializerSignature )
        {
            System.out.println("Signature type:    "+"Initializer");
        }
        if( sig instanceof MethodSignature )
        {
            System.out.println("Signature type:    "+"Method");
            System.out.println("   Return type: "+
                                    ((MethodSignature) sig).getReturnType());
        }
        if( sig instanceof FieldSignature )
        {
            System.out.println("Signature type:    "+"Field");
            System.out.println("    Field type:    "+
                                    ((FieldSignature) sig).getFieldType());
        }

        SourceLocation sl =  thisJoinPointStaticPart.getSourceLocation();
        System.out.println("Within type:       "+sl.getWithinType());
        System.out.println("File name:         "+sl.getFileName());
        System.out.println("Line:              "+sl.getLine());
        System.out.println("Column:            "+sl.getColumn());
    }
}
```

The aspect is now compiled and run with the class in Listing A.3.

LISTING A.3   APIMain.java Class

```
public class APIMain
{
    int i;

    public String exec(int a, String b)
                        throws InterruptedException, ClassNotFoundException
    {
        i=a;
        return "some text";
    }
```

LISTING A.3   Continued

```
    public static void main(String args[])
    {
        try
        {
            APIMain a = new APIMain();

            a.exec(3, "5.5");

            throw new IllegalAccessException("some text");
        }
        catch(Exception e)
        {
        }
    }
}
```

It describes all the join points, as shown in Listing A.4.

LISTING A.4   Output of APIAspect Aspect

```
******* staticinitialization(APIMain.<init>) *******
Target:        null
This:          null
Arguments:
Signature:     APIMain.<init>
Signature name: <init>
Declaring type: class APIMain
Signature type: Member
Signature type: Code
Signature type: Initializer
Within type:    class APIMain
File name:      APIMain.java
Line:          10
Column:        1


******* execution(void APIMain.main(String[])) *******
Target:        null
This:          null
Arguments:     [Ljava.lang.String;([Ljava.lang.String;@239137)
Signature:     void APIMain.main(String[])
Signature name: main
```

LISTING A.4   Continued

```
Declaring type: class APIMain
Signature type: Member
Signature type: Code
    Param type:  class [Ljava.lang.String;
    Param name:  args
Signature type: Method
    Return type: void
Within type:     class APIMain
File name:       APIMain.java
Line:            22
Column:          5


******* call(APIMain()) *******
Target:          null
This:            null
Arguments:
Signature:       APIMain()
Signature name: <init>
Declaring type: class APIMain
Signature type: Member
Signature type: Code
Signature type: Constructor
Within type:     class APIMain
File name:       APIMain.java
Line:            26
Column:          25


******* initialization(APIMain()) *******
Target:          APIMain@58610
This:            APIMain@58610
Arguments:
Signature:       APIMain()
Signature name: <init>
Declaring type: class APIMain
Signature type: Member
Signature type: Code
Signature type: Constructor
Within type:     class APIMain
File name:       APIMain.java
Line:            11
Column:          1
```

LISTING A.4   Continued

```
******* execution(APIMain.<init>) *******
Target:         APIMain@58610
This:           APIMain@58610
Arguments:
Signature:      APIMain.<init>
Signature name: <init>
Declaring type: class APIMain
Signature type: Member
Signature type: Code
Signature type: Initializer
Within type:    class APIMain
File name:      APIMain.java
Line:           10
Column:         1

******* execution(APIMain()) *******
Target:         APIMain@58610
This:           APIMain@58610
Arguments:
Signature:      APIMain()
Signature name: <init>
Declaring type: class APIMain
Signature type: Member
Signature type: Code
Signature type: Constructor
Within type:    class APIMain
File name:      APIMain.java
Line:           10
Column:         1

******* call(String APIMain.exec(int, String)) *******
Target:         null
This:           APIMain@58610
Arguments:      java.lang.Integer(3) java.lang.String(5.5)
Signature:      String APIMain.exec(int, String)
Signature name: exec
Declaring type: class APIMain
Signature type: Member
Signature type: Code
   Param type:  int
   Param name:  a
```

LISTING A.4   Continued

```
   Param type:  class java.lang.String
   Param name:  b
   Exception type: class java.lang.InterruptedException
   Exception type: class java.lang.ClassNotFoundException
Signature type: Method
   Return type: class java.lang.String
Within type:    class APIMain
File name:      APIMain.java
Line:           28
Column:         13

******* execution(String APIMain.exec(int, String)) *******
Target:         APIMain@58610
This:           APIMain@58610
Arguments:      java.lang.Integer(3) java.lang.String(5.5)
Signature:      String APIMain.exec(int, String)
Signature name: exec
Declaring type: class APIMain
Signature type: Member
Signature type: Code
   Param type:  int
   Param name:  a
   Param type:  class java.lang.String
   Param name:  b
   Exception type: class java.lang.InterruptedException
   Exception type: class java.lang.ClassNotFoundException
Signature type: Method
   Return type: class java.lang.String
Within type:    class APIMain
File name:      APIMain.java
Line:           16
Column:         5

******* set(int APIMain.i) *******
Target:         APIMain@58610
This:           APIMain@58610
Arguments:      java.lang.Integer(3)
Signature:      int APIMain.i
Signature name: i
Declaring type: class APIMain
Signature type: Member
```

LISTING A.4   Continued

```
Signature type: Field
     Field type: int
Within type:     class APIMain
File name:       APIMain.java
Line:            18
Column:          9


******* call(java.lang.IllegalAccessException(String)) *******
Target:          null
This:            null
Arguments:       java.lang.String(some text)
Signature:       java.lang.IllegalAccessException(String)
Signature name: <init>
Declaring type: class java.lang.IllegalAccessException
Signature type: Member
Signature type: Code
   Param type:  class java.lang.String
   Param name:  __0
Signature type: Constructor
Within type:     class APIMain
File name:       APIMain.java
Line:            30
Column:          19


******* handler(catch(Exception)) *******
Target:          null
This:            null
Arguments:       java.lang.IllegalAccessException(
                                  java.lang.IllegalAccessException: some text)
Signature:       catch(Exception)
Signature name:
Declaring type: class APIMain
Signature type: CatchClause
   Param type:  class java.lang.Exception
   Param name:  e
Within type:     class APIMain
File name:       APIMain.java
Line:            32
Column:      9
```

AspectJ Command-Line Tools

In this appendix I will describe the most frequently used parameters of the AspectJ compiler and doc generator.

The ajc Tool

The ajc tool is a compiler for the AspectJ language. It can be invoked by its wrapper script (ajc.bat for Windows operating systems or ajc shell script for Unix). It can also be invoked by using Java runtime because the compiler is written in Java and can be run directly by executing org.aspectj.tools.ajc.Main class (that is, its main() method) with the same set of parameters as for the wrapper script.

The general invocation format is as follows:

```
ajc [options] [file... | @file... | -arglist file...]
```

The ajc will compile files listed in its command line or files found in the list file. The list filename can be specified either by "@" symbol or -arglist command option.

ajc does not search the class path for the needed classes, so all source files must be specified in the command line, simultaneously.

ajc accepts the following options:

- -O   Turns optimization on with all the usual consequences: larger files and strange debugger behavior.

- -argfile *file*   Specifies the file that contains the list of filenames to be compiled, one filename per line.

- `-bootclasspath` *path*   Specifies the location of bootstrap classes used for cross-compiling the sources for different Java implementations.

- `-classpath` *path*   The paths for classes in the usual Java meaning.

- `-d` *dir*   Sets the output directory for `.class` files. The current directory is the default.

- `-emacssym`   Turns on symbol generation for the Emac development environment, so Emacs can navigate the source tree.

- `-encoding` *encoding*   Sets character encoding for the sources.

- `-extdirs` *path*   Specifies location of installed extensions.

- `-lenient`   Tells the compiler to be lenient with regard to the Java language.

- `-nocomments`   Instructs the compiler not to generate any comments when in `-preprocess` mode (see the following).

- `-preprocess`   Turns on the preprocessing mode, but no `.class` files are generated. Instead, the compiler compiles AspectJ sources into intermediate `.java` files and stops.

- `-strict`   Tells the compiler to be strict with regard to the Java language.

- `-usejavac`   Instructs the compiler to use regular `javac` to generate byte codes; the internal compiler will be used by default.

- `-verbose`   Produces a lot of messages as `ajc` is going along.

- `-version`   Prints the version information for the compiler.

- `-workingdir` *directory*   In `-usejavac` or `-preprocess` modes specifies the output directory for intermediate `.java` files. The default is `./ajworkingdir`.

`ajdoc`

The `ajdoc` tool generates API documentation in HTML format. It is based on the javadoc tool and accepts all the standard `javadoc` parameters (see `http://java.sun.com/j2se/1.3/docs/tooldocs/javadoc/index.html` for details). The general format of the command is

`ajdoc [options] [packagenames] [sourcefiles] [@files]`

The differences from the javadoc tool are as follows:

- ajdoc generates documentation for crosscuts, advices, and introductions.
- ajdoc adds links to the members affected by advices and introductions.
- ajdoc links introduced fields to corresponding introductions.
- ajdoc links advised methods to corresponding advices.
- ajdoc needs all the source files to be listed on the command line or included in list files.

C

Auxiliary Tools

This appendix describes all the other tools that were used in this book. All of them are easily available from the Internet, which was the only criterion for their selection—no endorsement is implied.

Tomcat

Tomcat is a Servlet/JSP container. It is a part of the Jakarta Project, which is an open-source project to provide Java-based tools developed in open and cooperative fashion. Tomcat 4 implements the Servlet 2.3 and JavaServer Pages 1.2 specifications, both available from

`http://www.jcp.org/aboutJava/communityprocess/final/jsr053`

Version 4.0.1 of Tomcat was used in this book; the software can be downloaded from

`http://jakarta.apache.org/builds/jakarta-tomcat-4.0/release/v4.0.1`

It is distributed under Apache Software License that can be examined at

`http://apache.org/LICENSE.`

After downloading, the software needs to be unpacked into its own directory, commonly denoted as `CATALINA_HOME` (don't ask). To run it, the `JAVA_HOME` environment variable has to be set, and it needs to point to the JDK installation directory. Tomcat can be started via its start-up script, which resides in `CATALINA_HOME/bin` subdirectory and is called either `startup.bat` (on Windows) or `startup.sh` (on Unix). A pair of shutdown scripts, predictably enough, performs the reverse operation.

The last part of the Tomcat's set-up process is to tell it where the example application is. To do this, the following XML fragment has to be inserted into `CATALINA_HOME/conf/server.xml` file

```
<Context path="/an" docBase="AspectNews" reloadable="true" debug="0"/>
```

It creates an application context for our example application and tells Tomcat two things. First, that the application will be accessed from Web browsers using prefix an on the URL. Second, that the application files will be located in the subdirectory called `AspectNews` of the application base directory, which is in `CATALINA_HOME/webapps/` unless configured otherwise.

There are many more configuration options for Tomcat, but this is sufficient to run the example application. The default port of the server is 8080, but it can be changed to a more convenient port 80 by finding and editing the connector configuration that listens to this port in the `CATALINA_HOME/conf/server.xml` file. It should look similar to this:

```
<Connector
className="org.apache.catalina.connector.http.HttpConnector"
port="8080"
minProcessors="5"
maxProcessors="75"
enableLookups="true"
redirectPort="8443"
acceptCount="10"
debug="0"
connectionTimeout="60000"
/>
```

After all this is done, the application can be accessed via the URL `http://localhost:8080/an` provided that the database was installed, configured, and loaded properly (see the next section).

MySQL Database

MySQL is the open source, relational database developed and marketed by a Swedish company MySQL AB. For the examples used in this book version 3.23.47 for Windows was used. It is available for download from one of the MySQL mirror sites around the globe; pick one at `http://mysql.com/downloads/mysql-3.23.html`.

MySQL is available either under GNU General Public License (GPL) or commercially directly from the MySQL AB. The full text of GPL is located at `http://www.gnu.org/copyleft/gpl.html`.

After obtaining and unpacking the distribution into some directory, the configuration file needs to be created (on Windows it is called `c:\winnt\my.ini`) that looks like this:

```
[mysqld]
basedir=D:/tools/mysql-3.23.47
datadir=D:/tools/mysql-3.23.47/data
```

After that, the database can be started via one of the executables in the `bin` directory of the distribution tree.

Initially, MySQL comes with no password for the root user, but it is strongly advised that you add one if you're planning to use the database for anything more than playing with the examples in this book. It is also prudent to create normal users for ordinary work, that is, users that do not have administrative privileges. Examples elsewhere in this book use a user `scott` with password `tiger`. As usual, there is more to database security than this, but, roughly, after user permissions have been taken care of, these are the steps to set up the MySQL database for use with the examples:

Connect to the database:

```
shell>mysql -u scott -ptiger
```

Create the database and exit:

```
mysql>create database an;
mysql>exit;
```

Create tables for the example application using the following command:

```
shell>mysql -u scott -ptiger an < scipt_name
```

In this command `script_name` should be one of the table creation scripts needed by the example application (shown in Listings C.1 through C.3 and also available online).

LISTING C.1   `users.sql` Script

```
CREATE TABLE users
(
        name VARCHAR(20),
        pass VARCHAR(20)
);

INSERT INTO users VALUES ('john','john');
INSERT INTO users VALUES ('bob', 'bob');
INSERT INTO users VALUES ('jack','jack');
```

LISTING C.2   `stories.sql` Script

```
CREATE TABLE stories
(
        category VARCHAR(50),
        body     TEXT
);

INSERT INTO stories VALUES ('HEALTH','Will we ...');
INSERT INTO stories VALUES ('HEALTH','Will the artificial ...');
INSERT INTO stories VALUES ('HEALTH','Will there be any ...');
INSERT INTO stories VALUES ('POLITICS', 'As 2002 gets under ...');
INSERT INTO stories VALUES ('POLITICS', 'With Democrats ...');
INSERT INTO stories VALUES ('POLITICS', 'Congress passed ...');
INSERT INTO stories VALUES ('ENTERTAINMENT','Who\'s going to ...');
INSERT INTO stories VALUES ('ENTERTAINMENT','Pop music is ...');
```

LISTING C.3   `preferences.sql` Script

```
CREATE TABLE preferences
(
        name     VARCHAR(20),
        category VARCHAR(50)
);

INSERT INTO preferences VALUES ('john','ENTERTAINMENT');
INSERT INTO preferences VALUES ('john','POLITICS');
INSERT INTO preferences VALUES ('bob', 'ENTERTAINMENT');
INSERT INTO preferences VALUES ('bob', 'POLITICS');
INSERT INTO preferences VALUES ('bob', 'HEALTH');
```

To use MySQL from Java, the JDBC driver is needed. One can be downloaded from
`http://mysql.com/downloads/api-jdbc.html`.

In this book, the MM.MySQL driver version 1.2c was used. This driver is a type IV
JDBC driver developed by Mark Matthews and distributed under GNU Lesser General
Public License. Licensing terms are available at
`http://www.gnu.org/copyleft/lesser.html`.

Ant

Apache Ant is a Java-based build tool from the Jakarta Project family. According to
its authors, "in theory it is kind of like make without make's wrinkles." While

leaving the validity of the claim solely on the Ant's authors' conscience, the tool has one distinct advantage: the platform portability inherited from Java. Ant version 1.4.1 was used in this book; the tool can be obtained from `http://jakarta.apache.org/builds/jakarta-ant/release/v1.4.1/`.

As part of the Jakarta Project, Ant is also distributed under Apache Software License (see `http://www.apache.org/LICENSE`).

After unpacking the distribution, you need to set `JAVA_HOME` environment variable to your Java installation directory and, on some platforms, `ANT_HOME` to where you have installed Ant. Ant's `bin` directory can be added to your path for convenience, but it is not required.

D

Quick Language Reference

In this appendix we will list main syntax elements of the AspectJ language in Backus-Naur form. Because the AspectJ language is based on Java, only the differentiating constructs of the AspectJ language are presented—that is, there is no point in describing the syntax of Java itself.

Aspect

```
aspect_declaration
    ::=
    { modifier } [privileged] "aspect" identifier {aspect_association}
    [ "dominates" type_pattern ]
    [ "extends" class_name | aspect_name ]
    [ "implements" interface_name { "," interface_name } ]
    "{"
        { method_declaration }
        { constructor_declaration }
        { variable_declaration }
        { static_initializer }
        { pointcut }
        { advice }
        { introduction }
    "}"
```

Aspect Association

```
aspect_association
    ::=
    ["issingleton"]
    | "perthits(pointcut)"
    | "pertarget(pointcut)"
    | "percflow(pointcut)"
    | "percflowbelow(pointcut)"
```

Type Patterns

```
type_pattern
    ::=
    type_name_pattern
    |( "!" type_pattern )
    |( "(" type_pattern ")" )
    |( type_pattern "+" )
    |( type_pattern "[]" )
    |( type_pattern "&&" type_pattern )
    |( type_pattern "||" type_pattern )

type_name_pattern
    ::=
    "*"
    | ( "a..z,A..Z,$,0..9,*,.,'..'" )
```

```
id_name_pattern
    ::=
    "*"
    | ( "a..z,A..Z,$,0..9,*" )
```

Advice

```
advice
    ::=
    before_advice
    | after_advice
    | around_advice

before_advice
    ::=
    "before" "(" [ parameter_list ] ")" : pointcut
    "{"
        { statement }
    "}"

after_advice
    ::=
    "after" "(" [ parameter_list ] ")"
        ["throwing" [parameter]] | ["returning" [parameter]] : pointcut
    "{"
        { statement }
    "}"

around_advice
    ::=
    type "around" "(" [ parameter_list ] ")"
        ["throws" type_list]: pointcut
    "{"
        { statement }
    "}"
```

Pointcut Designators

```
signature
    ::=
    { modifier } type_pattern type_pattern ["." id_name_pattern]
                                "(" type_pattern { "," type_pattern } ")"
pointcut
    ::=
```

```
    "call" "(" signature ")"
  | "execution" "(" signature ")"
  | "initialization" "(" signature ")"
  | "handler" "(" type_pattern ")"
  | "get" "(" signature ")"
  | "set" "(" signature ")"
  | "staticinitialization" "(" type_pattern ")"
  | "this" "(" type_pattern ")"
  | "target" "(" type_pattern ")"
  | "args" "(" type_pattern { "," type_pattern } ")"
  | "within" "(" type_pattern ")"
  | "withincode" "(" signature ")"
  | "cflow" "(" pointcut ")"
  | "cflowbelow" "(" pointcut ")"
  | "if" "(" expression ")"
  | "!" pointcut
  | pointcut "&&" pointcut
  | pointcut "||" pointcut
  | "(" pointcut ")"
```

Introduction

```
introduction
   ::=
   (
     [ modifiers ] type type_pattern "." id "(" parameter_list ")"
    "{"
       { statement }
    "}"
   )
  | ( "abstract" [ modifiers ] type type_pattern "." id "("
                                          parameter_list ")" ";" )
  | (
     [ modifiers ] type type_pattern "." "new" "(" parameter_list ")"
    "{"
       { statement }
    "}"
    )
  | ( [ modifiers ] type type_pattern "." id [ "=" expression ] ";" )
  | ( "declare" "parents" ":" type_pattern "extends" type_list ";" )
  | ( "declare" "parents" ":" type_pattern "implements" type_list ";" )
  | ( "declare" "warning" ":" pointcut string ";" )
  | ( "declare" "error" ":" pointcut string ";" )
  | ( "declare" "soft" ":" type_pattern ":" pointcut ";" )
```

E

AspectJ Project

In this appendix I will describe the AspectJ project, and the ways to get in touch with AspectJ community.

Project at PARC

The AspectJ project was started on August 1998 at the Palo Alto Research Center of Xerox Corporation. It is funded by Xerox and Defense Advanced Research Projects Agency. The stated goals are

> "...to make aspect-oriented programming technology available to a wide range of programmers, to build and support an AspectJ user community, and to use the experiences of that user community to improve both AspectJ in particular and aspect-oriented programming in general."

The development team started on a domain-specific aspect language, and then transitioned to a Java-based one. Since release 0.7, the AspectJ project has been published as open source. The first official version, 1.0 (on which this book is based), was released in November 2001.

On a goal list for the near future are two major changes: incremental compilation for release 1.1, and an ability to crosscut not only source files, but also compiled bytecodes for version 2.0.

Contact Information

The main project Web site is http://aspectj.org.

At the time of this writing, the project team consists of Gregor Kiczales (Project Leader), Ron Bodkin, Bill Griswold,

Erik Hilsdale, Jim Hugunin, Wes Isberg, and Mik Kersten. The project is physically hosted at Xerox PARC, the snail-mail address is

Palo Alto Research Center
3333 Coyote Hill Road
Palo Alto, CA 94304

General inquiries should be directed to this email: info@aspectj.org. The development team can be contacted by sending an email to support@aspectj.org.

Community Participation and Support

To the best of my knowledge, the commercial support for AspectJ is not yet offered, but that might change in the future. There are, however, numerous options for community support and participation.

The AspectJ FAQ helps to address the most pressing problems. It is available on the main Web site at http://aspectj.org/doc/dist/faq.html.

The AspectJ team maintains two mailing lists: users@aspectj.org for AspectJ-related discussions, and announce@aspectj.org for announcing major news related to the project. Subscription to both lists is available from the Web site.

An archive of all previous discussions on the users' mailing list is available for viewing or download. Please, search it and read the FAQ before sending a help request to the list.

Finally, the Web site provides a form-based interface to the bug database where known bugs can be searched, and newly discovered bugs reported. Again, use it first before posting a question to the whole users' list.

F

References

Gamma, Erich, Richard Helm, Ralph Johnson, and John Vlissides. 1995. *Design Patterns: Elements of Reusable Object-Oriented Software*. Addison-Wesley. This modern technical classic is also known as the "Gang-of-Four" book. It introduced a format for describing design patterns and provided a fresh look at what today's programmers are doing every day.

Kiczales, Gregor, John Lamping, Anurag Mendhekar, Chris Maeda, Cristina Videira Lopes, Jean-Marc Loingtier, and John Irwin. June 1997. "Aspect-Oriented Programming." Proceedings of the European Conference on Object-Oriented Programming (ECOOP), Finland. Springer-Verlag LNCS 1241. This is one of the early publications on aspect-oriented programming that states its major principles. The paper is available from the AspectJ Web site at
`http://aspectj.org/documentation/papersAndSlides/ECO OP1997-AOP.pdf`.

Kiselev, Ivan. November 2000. "Resource Pooling in Java." *Java Developers Journal*: 22-28. This article contains more or less detailed discussion about resource pool implementations. The reason it is cited here (besides vanity, of course) is that I am not aware of any other such discussion widely available—this was the reason I wrote the article in the first place.

Meyer, Bertrand. 1988. *Object-Oriented Software Construction*. Prentice Hall. Everyone doing object-oriented programming should read this classic book. It spells out, among other things, design-by-contract principles. The newer edition is available.

Sun Microsystems, Inc. "Proposal: A Simple Assertion Facility for the Java™ Programming Language." `http://www.jcp.org/content/main/jsr/detail/ materials/asrt_prop.html`. This is the proposal for Java language extension to include an assertion statement. It will be included in the upcoming 1.4 release of the Java's SDK.

————. October 2000. JDBC™ 3.0 Specification, Proposed Final Draft 4. `http://java.sun.com/products/jdbc/download.html`. This page describes the latest and greatest (at the time of this writing) version of the JDBC spec. The API will be included in SDK v.1.4, but actual driver availability will be at the publishers' discretion.

————. September 17, 2001. Java™ Servlet API Specification, Version: 2.3. `http://www.jcp.org/aboutJava/communityprocess/final/jsr053/`. This document describes the servlet specification now in common use.

G

Glossary

abstract aspect   An aspect that contains abstract point-cuts.

abstract pointcut   A pointcut without a body. It can be declared only inside abstract aspects.

advice   A language construct that contains code that will run when the corresponding join point is reached.

aspect   A programming module that contains the implementation of a crosscutting concern.

aspect-oriented programming (AOP)   A way of building information systems where common domain-crossing design decisions are modularized in the separate layers of code.

crosscutting concerns   The design problems that exhibit themselves globally across functional- and object-programming modules.

join point   A well-defined execution point in a program.

pointcut   A set of join points specified by a pointcut designator.

pointcut designator (PCD)   A language construct that identifies a pointcut.

primitive pointcut   A pointcut that does not contain any pointcut expressions.

runtime exception   A descendant of the `java.lang.RuntimeException` class.

signature   A collection of names, types, and identifiers that allows identification of a method.

signature pattern   A wild-card expression that can match a collection of signatures and can be used in pointcuts.

softened exception   A runtime exception of type `org.aspectj.lang.SoftException` that represents an original program's exception wrapped for the purpose of avoiding Java compile time type checking.

static crosscutting   A number of AspectJ language facilities to support changing the static object structure of a Java program.

thisJoinPoint   Compiler-generated special variable that provides the join point–specific context information to an advice.

type pattern   A wild-card expression that can match a collection of types, which can then be used in the AspectJ language in place of a single type.

Index

Symbols

A

B

C

D

G

H

M

N

O

P

Q-R

S

How can we make this index more useful? Email us at indexes@samspublishing.com

Other Related Titles